# THE CEREDIGION AND SNOWDONIA COAST PATHS

### THE WALES COAST PATH
### FROM PORTHMADOG TO ST DOGMAELS

## About the Author

Although brought up in northwest Kent, where he enjoyed walking in the countryside from an early age, John B Jones has lived most of his life in the Derbyshire Peak District. He has walked extensively in the British Isles and abroad, including completing more than 25 long-distance trails; climbing all 214 'Wainwright' hills in the Lake District twice and climbing all the Scottish Munros, Corbetts and Grahams (over 720 hills and mountains). He is the author of the original Her Majesty's Stationery Office (HMSO) guide to the Offa's Dyke Path and has written a number of local authority walking guides.

With Welsh ancestry on his father's side John has a great affinity with Wales, and there are few corners of the country he has not explored.

For over 30 years John worked in the Greater Manchester area with responsibility for a large derelict land and environmental improvement programme, and in the management of sizeable areas of countryside. Besides his walking activities, John is also a voluntary countryside ranger and an accomplished classical pianist.

# THE CEREDIGION AND SNOWDONIA COAST PATHS

### THE WALES COAST PATH
### FROM PORTHMADOG TO ST DOGMAELS

by John B Jones

2 POLICE SQUARE, MILNTHORPE, CUMBRIA LA7 7PY
www.cicerone.co.uk

© John B Jones 2014
First edition 2014
ISBN: 978 1 85284 738 8

Printed by KHL Printing, Singapore.
A catalogue record for this book is available from the British Library.
The sketch maps are based on information compiled by the author.
All photographs are by the author unless otherwise stated.

## Acknowledgments

I would like to record my sincere thanks to Roger Williams, whose knowledge of the birdlife along the coast was invaluable; to my walking friends of many years, Ted Roskell, Phil Murnaghan and Alan Ford for their company on parts of the walk; and to Hilary Matthews for her wonderful hospitality while this book was being researched.

## Advice to Readers

While every effort is made by our authors to ensure the accuracy of guidebooks as they go to print, changes can occur during the lifetime of an edition. If we know of any, there will be an Updates tab on this book's page on the Cicerone website (www.cicerone.co.uk), so please check before planning your trip. We also advise that you check information about such things as transport, accommodation and shops locally. Even rights of way can be altered over time. We are always grateful for information about any discrepancies between a guidebook and the facts on the ground, sent by email to info@cicerone.co.uk or by post to Cicerone, 2 Police Square, Milnthorpe LA7 7PY, United Kingdom.

*Front cover:* The view north from near Craig y Delyn (Day 9)

# CONTENTS

**Route symbols on OS map extracts**

official route                      start point

proposed official route            finish point
(not yet available)

alternative route                  alternative start point

direction of walk                  alternative finish point

                                   sketch map area

For full OS symbols key see OS maps

In the above key, 'official route' means the designated route of the Wales Coast Path; 'proposed official route' means that the official route was not available at the time of publication of this guidebook; 'alternative route' means both official alternatives to the main route, such as at times of high tides, and alternatives suggested by the author.

# Sketch map key

| | |
|---|---|
| (symbol) | start point |
| (symbol) | finish point |
| (symbol) | road (fenced; unfenced; unfenced on one side) |
| (symbol) | track/lane (fenced; unfenced; unfenced on one side) |
| (symbol) | route |
| (symbol) | alternative route |
| (symbol) | other paths |
| (symbol) | field boundary |
| (symbol) | railway |
| (symbol) | narrow gauge railway |
| (symbol) | river/stream |
| 75 (symbol) | contours (at 25-metre intervals) |
| (symbol) | wood/copse |
| (symbol) | footbridge |
| (symbol) | gate |
| (symbol) | stile |
| (symbol) | buildings |
| (symbol) | church/chapel |
| (symbol) | caravan/chalet park |

## Shoreline features

| | | | |
|---|---|---|---|
| MHW | mean high water | (symbol) | cliffs |
| MLW | mean low water | (symbol) | rock ledges |
| (symbol) | shingle/pebbles | (symbol) | salt marsh |
| (symbol) | sand | (symbol) | dunes |

The view up the coast north of Llanrhystud (Day 10)

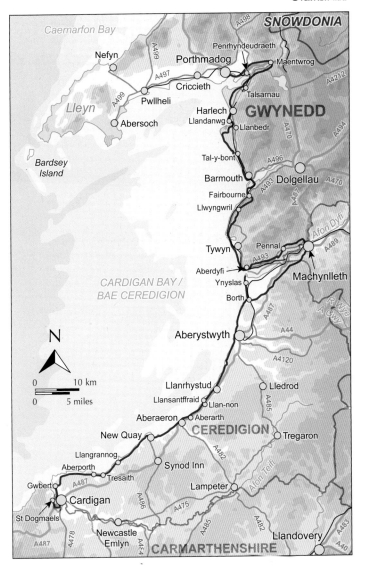

The long sweep of sands at Traeth Penbryn (Day 14)

# INTRODUCTION

*A breezy day in the dunes of Morfa Harlech (Day 3)*

By turns rugged and gently contoured, sweeping and intimate, exciting and atmospheric, the coast of Wales down Cardigan Bay, from the end of the Lleyn Peninsula Coastal Path to the start of the Pembrokeshire Coast Path, makes for an inspiring walk. This guide covers the splendid and varied section of the Wales Coast Path along the Snowdonia coast, around the Dyfi Estuary and down the Ceredigion coast – a distance of 233km (145 miles).

The route follows long sandy beaches, high rugged cliffs and steep-sided cwms; you walk beside salt-marshes, stride over coastal plains, wander through the margins of Snowdonia's coastal hills and crunch along pebble storm beaches. And there are great views: on clear days, especially from the central parts of Cardigan Bay, you can see the whole sweep of the coast from Bardsey Island to Strumble Head, backed by the mountains of Snowdonia in the north and rolling green hills in the south.

There are beautiful inland routes around the estuaries of Traeth Bach and the Dyfi, many attractive settlements to pass through and much of historic interest. A fascinating geology is laid bare in the different rock strata and landforms, and there is a rich and immensely varied natural history.

*Cnicht and the Moelwyns, as seen from the Cob at Porthmadog (Day 1)*

While here and there the walk passes stark caravan sites, your abiding memories will be of a superb coast.

## THE WALES COAST PATH/ LLWYBR ARFORDIR CYMRU

On 5 May 2012 the Wales Coast Path was officially opened: a full 1400km (870 miles), from the outskirts of Chester in the north to Chepstow in the south, making it the first long-distance trail in the world to follow an entire national coastline. While the path incorporates existing coastal routes (including the Pembrokeshire Coast Path, the Lleyn Peninsula Coastal Path, the Anglesey Coastal Path and the more recent Ceredigion Coast Path), many new sections were needed. For the whole Wales Coast Path to have been created in such a remarkably short timescale is a magnificent achievement. Visit www. walescoastpath.gov.uk for more information.

## THE LLŶN TO PEMBROKESHIRE: THE ROUTE IN SUMMARY

**The Snowdonia Coast Path: Porthmadog to Aberdyfi**
This is not an official title but a name of convenience; since most of the route is within Snowdonia National Park it seems appropriate. The truly coastal sections tend to be along huge sandy beaches, while the remainder is through nearby hill country or across the coastal plains. Until you get to Harlech you would be forgiven for thinking you were not on a coast path, as the route takes you

well inland via Maentwrog (although the new road and cycleway between Penrhyndeudraeth and Llandecwyn, replacing the unsuitable toll road, could be used as a shortcut). However, the Maentwrog loop is a fine wooded section, with great views of a number of the Snowdonia peaks. The path then – following the coastal plain of Ardudwy, via saltmarshes and fields to Harlech – reaches the sea proper. Alternating between sandy beach and inland routes, it arrives at Tal-y-bont. Rather than taking the official main road route to Barmouth, consider either an enjoyable beach walk (low tide only) or a fine hill alternative on part of the Ardudwy Way. South of the Mawddach Estuary the path lies back from the sea through hill country, a splendid section. It ends along the vast beach from Tywyn to Aberdyfi.

**The Dyfi Estuary: Aberdyfi to Borth**

A long inland loop through the countryside on either side of the Dyfi Estuary via Machynlleth (the lowest road crossing point) takes the coast path through beautiful hill country, with lovely views, returning to the coast at Borth.

**The Ceredigion Coast Path: Ynyslas to Cardigan**

Promoted by Ceredigion County Council, particularly in association with the Ramblers and Aberystwyth Conservation Volunteers (who assisted with much of the physical improvement work), the Ceredigion Coast Path (www.ceredigioncoastpath.org.uk) was funded under the EU's Objective 1 programme for West Wales and the Valleys and was officially opened on 3 July 2008 by Jane Davidson AM,

*The Dyfi, seen from the ridge road (Day 7)*

13

the Welsh Assembly Government Environment, Sustainability and Housing Minister.

The path starts at the flat lands at Ynyslas and joins the Wales Coast Path at Borth. Over a distance of just short of 100km (60 miles), it links Ynyslas with Cardigan (Aberteifi) on the Teifi Estuary, following some of Wales' finest and most varied coast. It is quite different in character from the Snowdonia section: for the first time on the route there are extensive cliffs and the walking becomes much more truly coastal. The path runs magnificently over the cliffs to Aberystwyth and Llanrhystud, then an easy section along a narrow coastal plain leads to a long stretch of wonderfully rugged coastline, which is followed via Aberaeron, New Quay and Aberporth

all the way to Mwnt before the way turns inland along the Teifi Estuary to Cardigan. The path follows many sections of pre-existing and often improved rights of way, as well as a number of specially created sections.

### Cardigan to St Dogmaels

A short link on the south side of the estuary, via field paths and roads, leads to St Dogmaels and the official start of the Pembrokeshire Coast Path.

### THE STORY IN THE ROCKS

One of the delights of the coast path is its ever-changing scenery, resulting from the varied underlying geology.

Between Porthmadog and a little north of Broad Water you encounter the oldest rocks along the path. These

*An outcrop of Aberystwyth Grits at Allt-wen, south of Aberystwyth (Day 9)*

Undercut glacial cliffs near Mynachdy'r-graig (Day 10)

are called greywackes: hard, dark sandstones, alternating with softer slate and mudstones, formed 544 to 510 million years ago during the Cambrian period. Folded into a dome (the Harlech Dome), much eroded since its first formation, they rise from the coast towards the Rhinogs.

Subsequently the landmass that included Wales drifted north some 3000km (1865 miles) from the southern regions of the planet. Mudstones, siltstones and sandstones formed during this time occur along the coast between the Teifi and Ynys Lochtyn near Llangrannog.

Between Ynys Lochtyn and Borth the rocks of the later Silurian period comprise great thicknesses of greywackes, formed in fast-moving currents. The larger sand grains would

settle out first, with finer muds on top, a sequence repeated many times and seen in layer upon layer of alternating strata in the cliffs. Most striking of all, between Cwmtydu and Borth, are the so-called Aberystwyth Grits, nowadays considerably contorted as a result of mountain-building forces.

South of Tal-y-bont to Llanaber, the path runs over much younger clays, silts, sands and gravels formed a mere 55 to five million years ago.

The land we see today has been modified by erosion and glaciation. As the ice retreated, and especially with the last retreat about 12,000 years ago, large amounts of glacial moraine and till were left behind, of such quantity as to overspread the low-lying coastal tracts. New stretches of coastal plain were formed,

*Seen across a shimmering sea, Pendinaslochdyn appears in silhouette (Day 13)*

leaving former cliff lines inland. You can see this in the coastal strip between Aberaeron and Llanrhystud, for example. In some places the glacial debris is of such depth that it has formed its own coastal cliffs, such as at Llansantffraid. At Wallog, moraine forms the remarkable bank of Sarn Gynfelyn, stretching way out to sea, a survivor of thousands of years of tides and storms. Further up the coast, under the sea, lies the similar bank of Sarn Badrig.

At some places, such as off the coast of Borth, evidence of former land lies in the remains of submerged peat banks and old tree stumps still in their original positions, visible at low tide.

The processes of erosion and deposition are never-ending. We can see where the coastline is being changed today by the silting-up of the estuaries, or where marsh has formed and become vegetated, such as in the vast raised bog of Cors Fochno near Borth. And we can marvel at the huge dune systems formed in the last few hundred years, often as windblown sand has gained a toehold on the pebbles and gravels carried north up the coast by longshore drift.

## HISTORY

### Early settlers

By the time melting ice had finally cut Britain off from the rest of mainland Europe in about 5000BC, early colonists had already arrived on these islands. The first to leave visible evidence on the landscape, during the period from about 4000BC to 3000BC, were the Neolithic peoples. A number of Neolithic burial chambers are to be found in Gwynedd, a fine example being at Dyffryn Ardudwy. A number of stone circles, several near the coast, date from this time through to about 2000BC, as civilisation moved into the Bronze Age.

The Celts, who arrived in Wales from about 600BC, were warlike and had a culture steeped in legend. Their language (the various tribes speaking different versions of the same tongue) gave the basis for modern Welsh. The latter part of the first millennium BC saw the development of numerous hill forts, such as at Pendinas above Aberystwyth and at Pendinaslochdyn near Llangrannog.

### The Roman invasion

The Roman invasion of Britain from AD43 made relatively little impact on West Wales. There was known to be one fort, near the path at Pennal, but roads were largely absent and the Celtic peoples carried on their way of life much as before.

### After the Romans

The history of West Wales after the Romans departed is often shrouded in mystery. Irish tribes began to settle here; then, according to tradition, early in the fifth century one Cunedda and his eight sons came from Southern Scotland, subjugating the Irish settlers and imposing the Welsh (Brythonic) dialect of the Celts. It is perhaps no mere coincidence, then, that the conquered areas bear the names of Cunedda's sons. Dunawd, for instance, is said to have given his name to Dunoding (an area that included the coast

*St Crannog watches over Llangrannog village (Day 14)*

between present-day Porthmadog and Barmouth, the land of Ardudwy); Ceredig to Ceredigion, and Merion (the son of Tyrion, who had already died) to Meirionydd between the Dwyryd and Machynlleth. These are some of the oldest names in Wales.

At about this time, in the fifth and sixth centuries, there was a growth of monastic communities associated with powerful families, comprising a church and simple dwellings within an enclosure (a *llan*). Here religious men led a life of prayer and frugality. Along the route of the coast path the most famous of these men was Padarn at Llanbadarn (on the edge of present-day Aberystwyth), this llan later developing into the abbey and important bishopric of Llanbadarn Fawr. Many disciples who came to these llans went on to set up further churches, associated with the founder. Thus of the St David foundations there is Llannon, named after David's mother St Non, and Llangrannog, named after St David's grandfather Carannog.

## The Norman Conquest and the Wars of Independence

In the following centuries various attempts were made to create a wider unity in Wales, as, for instance, by Rhodri Mawr (844–878), his grandson Hywel Dda (c900–950) and others, but without long-term success.

A major change to the political map came with the arrival of the Normans, although in West Wales the conquest did not fully happen until the time of Henry I (who reigned from 1100 until 1135), when, for example, he gave Ceredigion to the powerful Richard fitz Gilbert de Clare, who built the castles at Cardigan and Llanbadarn. In the succeeding centuries the history of West Wales is complex as various rulers arose to drive back the Normans, only to be overthrown themselves.

Among them, towards the end of the 12th century, was Llewelyn the Great, who by 1234 controlled all of North Wales. After his death Henry III once more took control of many of the Welsh territories, including Llanbadarn. But by 1257 Llewelyn's grandson, Llewelyn ap Gruffydd, sought to restore the former position, notably in the two wars of 1276–1277 and 1282–1283. With Llewelyn's death on 11 December 1282, defeat was on hand. The royal army advanced, taking, among other places, Ceredigion. Edward I, already building new castles elsewhere in Wales (as well as strengthening a number of existing Welsh castles, such as Llanbadarn) now initiated a further phase of castle-building, including Harlech Castle.

Houses of most of the monastic orders had come into Wales by now, paramount being the Cistercian house of Strata Florida, inland at Pontrhydfendigaid, under the patronage of the lords of Deheubarth and holding significant areas of coastal land at Dolaeron, Morfa Mawr and Morfa Bychan. Whitland Abbey in

Carmarthenshire held coastal land at Porth Fechan (by Aberporth) and at Esgair Saith (by Tresaith). Cardigan and Llanbadarn were Benedictine foundations.

## The Glyndŵr revolt

At Machynlleth the coast path reaches the place most closely associated with Owain Glyndŵr. He was born in around 1354, was well-read, spoke English, knew the legal system and became a soldier loyal to the English king.

Wales was turbulent in the 14th century, with much anger still emanating from Edward I's subjugation of the country and from more recent swingeing taxes. The revolt arose from a local dispute with the English Lord Grey of Ruthin, who had apparently seized some of Glyndŵr's land. The courts failing to back him, Glyndŵr took up the cudgels and, having been declared Prince of Wales in 1400 by the insurrectionists, first attacked Ruthin with some 4000 men, then moved on through Oswestry to Welshpool.

Henry IV's two expeditions of 1402 to quell the uprising, and the introduction of punitive laws, simply caused an escalation of the revolt. By 1403 Glyndŵr controlled much of Wales, and in 1404 he was crowned ruler of a free Wales in Machynlleth.

Glyndŵr, keen to form alliances with other sovereign nations, courted the allegiance of the French king and set out to demonstrate, in the *Pennal Letter*, his allegiance to the Pope in Avignon. But inexorably the Welsh

*Machynlleth's Parliament House is a Grade I listed building (Day 7)*

19

This monument to Owain Glyndŵr stands in the park at Machynlleth (Day 8)

were overcome, and by 1407 the rebellion was fading. Glyndŵr fled into hiding and died, it is believed, in Herefordshire in about 1416. He was unquestionably a man of vision, for had the rebellion succeeded some believe Wales could at that time have had its own church and university. However, the Welsh economy was left in a parlous state, and many churches and at least 40 towns had suffered significant damage.

### Henry Tudor

The next historic event of note along the coast was the progress through Wales of Henry Tudor (the future Henry VII). It was the usurpation of the English throne by Richard III, after the death of Edward IV (1483), which brought Henry into prominence. Landing at Dale in Pembrokeshire on 7 July 1485, and with considerable support from the Welsh, he made rapid progress up the coast, arriving at Cardigan on 9 August, Llanbadarn on 10 August and Machynlleth the following day, on his way to Bosworth.

### The uniting of England and Wales

Under Henry VIII's Act of Union of 1536, initiating the uniting of Wales and England into a single state, the boundaries of the modern shires were largely determined by those of the old Welsh divisions. Merionethshire included the coastal plain of the old lands of Ardudwy, while Cardiganshire (as the area was now called) conformed surprisingly closely to the ancient lands of Ceredig, son of Cunedda, a remarkable continuity down the centuries.

*Second World War tank traps still line the beach at Fairbourne (Day 5)*

21

Sea pinks and birdsfoot trefoil are found along the coast path during the spring and summer months

## WILDLIFE

The varied habitats found along the coast path – the cliffs, dunes, salt-marshes and woodlands, as well as the sea itself – support a wonderful array of plants and creatures. There are several nationally important nature reserves, and large tracts of the coast have been afforded special protection. Stretching 30km (19 miles) out to sea, the whole section from the Llŷn to Clarach has been designated as a Special Area of Conservation, as has the section from Aberarth to Cemaes Head in Pembrokeshire. The Dyfi Estuary has been designated as Wales' only International Biosphere, with protection for the dunes, the extensive raised bog of Cors Fochno and other habitats.

Four sections of the Ceredigion coast (from Borth to Clarach, Twll Twrw to Llanrhystud, New Quay to Tresaith and Pen-Peles to Gwbert)

have also been designated as Heritage Coast and are managed to conserve their natural beauty.

Offshore, Cardigan Bay supports an amazing variety of marine plants and animals, from bottlenose dolphins to the humble reef-building worm. Along the coastal margins, the sandbanks, reefs and caves are also hugely important for wildlife, with their attendant populations of grey seals and lampreys.

From spring into summer a wealth of wildflowers thrives along the cliff sections of the path, including orchids, sea pinks, birdsfoot trefoil, thrift and bladder campion, with drifts of bluebells here and there. The common gorse is prolific, adding splashes of bright yellow to the landscape in the season. Butterflies also do well in these areas, and the cliffs are important breeding grounds for birds such as the razorbill, fulmar, guillemot and kittiwake, as well as gulls, and there are also populations of chough. Certain rocks are favourite places for cormorants to perch and hang their wings out to dry. You would be unlucky not to see red kite along the coast either side of Llanrhystud.

By contrast the shingle beaches may seem devoid of life, but a closer look will reveal plants such as the sea campion and sea holly thriving. The shingly flats near Broad Water, where the Dysynni reaches the sea, are a good place to see sandwich terns, eider ducks and turnstones, especially at high tide.

Large tracts of the extensive dunes, especially along the Snowdonia coast, are National Nature Reserves, owing to their rich wildlife (including orchids) and their butterflies, other insects and birds such as the shelduck and curlew.

The path crosses several areas of saltmarsh and runs beside estuarine flats such as those of Traeth Bach, the Mawddach and Dyfi – good food sources for waders and winter migrants such as redshank, wigeon and oystercatcher. In the Traeth Bach area look out all year round for the red-breasted merganser, and in winter for peregrine falcons, whooper swans and water pipits. Osprey have been breeding in the area for several years and you may be lucky enough to spot one diving for fish. The grasshopper warbler and common whitethroat can sometimes be heard around the Mawddach Estuary, and offshore from the Dyfi Estuary in winter you may spot red-throated divers, long-tailed ducks and the common scoter.

The fragrant, bell-shaped flowers of bladder campion

The various areas of woodland (found, for instance, in the coastal cwms and dingles) are locally important for wildlife, while much of the more extensive Maentwrog oakwood above the Afon Dwyryd has been designated as a Special Area of Conservation, supporting hundreds of species of mosses, liverworts and lichens, rare bats, and birds such as the pied flycatcher, redstart and wood warbler.

## COMMERCE ALONG THE COAST

### The boatbuilding era

All along the coast (and especially south of the Dyfi) from the later decades of the 18th century and through the 19th century, boatbuilding was a thriving industry even in the smallest of settlements and least promising locations, as the roads were in a poor state and goods were often transported by sea.

Hundreds of vessels of many types, such as smacks, schooners and brigs, were built at this time and the economies of Cardigan, Aberystwyth and Aberaeron were largely based on this industry. The vessels plied their trade not just up and down the coast, but also across the Atlantic. Limestone and timber were major imports, and slate (especially from ports north of Machynlleth) was the main exported commodity. Wherever there was boatbuilding, so secondary trades went hand in hand, including rope and sailmaking, insurance and customs.

The advent of steam power, and of iron as a ship-building material, meant a decline in demand for the timber-built sail-powered boats; and the arrival of the railway, which

*A well-preserved limekiln at Cwmtydu (Day 13)*

A plaque near the Urdd Centre marks the official opening of the Ceredigion Coast Path (Day 13)

enabled goods to be moved more easily by land, led to a wholesale demise of the industry. By the beginning of the 20th century it had largely disappeared.

## The limestone industry

Limestone was a significant import in the 19th century. It was burnt in kilns to produce quicklime for use in building mortar, and for 'sweetening' the agricultural land; all along the coast – again, especially south of the Dyfi – there are limekilns, sometimes in quite out-of-the-way places.

At the kilns the limestone was crushed, usually by hand, to a uniform size and built up into a dome, with alternate layers of coal inside the furnace on a grate above the 'eye' of the kiln (the air intake). The kilns were all roughly the same size, as

this accommodated the optimum size of fire: any bigger and the coal and limestone would collapse under their own weight. Lime-burning was not only thirsty work but also unhealthy because of the smoke and fumes.

The coming of the railways meant that lime could be transported around the country more easily by larger manufacturers, so the small-scale individual limekilns became unprofitable and fell out of use.

## The slate industry

Thousands of tonnes of slate per year were won from vast galleries in the hills of North Wales, particularly during the 19th and into the 20th century, with tramways and narrow gauge railways built to bring it to the coast for export. Serving the Rheidol Valley mines, a railway went down from

25

*Walkers on one of the steep slopes north of Llanrhystud (Day 10)*

Devil's Bridge to Aberystwyth carrying slate and zinc. This is now the famous Vale of Rheidol Railway. From near Abergynolwen, slate from the Bryn Eglwys Quarry went to Tywyn on the Talyllyn Railway. And from the vast slate area around Blaenau Ffestiniog, the Ffestiniog Railway linked to the coast at Porthmadog.

## Tourism

As the boatbuilding, limestone and slate industries declined, partly as a result of the arrival of the railway, it was the railway itself that prompted the growth of seaside resorts. Tourism remains a vital part of the economy of the area, based on its proximity to Snowdonia, on attractions such as the narrow gauge railways and on the magnificent coast.

## WALKING THE CEREDIGION AND SNOWDONIA COAST PATHS

### How long will it take?

Strong walkers could complete the full walk in just less than two weeks, averaging 22km (14 miles) a day. This would leave little time to wander through some of the settlements or visit the attractions along the way. Averaging about 16km (10 miles) a day, the walk would take you 15 days. It is also worth considering building in 'rest days' in order to visit, say, Harlech Castle, or ride one or more of the narrow gauge railways (see Visitor attractions, below). With conveniently spaced settlements, good links to public transport and available accommodation, the path could easily be broken down into shorter sections, giving time to explore and enjoy the scenery and the wildlife. For this you might need to allow about three weeks, possibly split between more than one holiday. It would also be perfectly possible to base yourself in one place for a few days and use public transport to reach the start of, and to return from, each day's walk (see Appendix A and Appendix B).

### How strenuous is it?

It is all too easy to underestimate the amount of climbing involved in much of the coastal walking in the British Isles. While long stretches of the Snowdonia Coast Path (being alongside saltmarshes or along sandy beaches) enable a fast pace, there are also some big ascents, especially

between Maentwrog and Llandecwyn and on the routes out of Fairbourne and Llwyngwril, and also on the hill alternative between Tal-y-bont and Barmouth (Day 4).

The Ceredigion Coast Path is a surprisingly challenging walk overall, with many ups and downs and some big days, requiring a good level of fitness.

### Alternative routes:
### high tide routes and other options

At Borth and at New Quay it is possible to follow the beach at low or falling tide, and there are official alternative routes for when the tide is high. Between Cwmtydu and Ynys Lochtyn (Day 13) there is an official inland alternative for those who wish to avoid the exposed coastal path.

*Allt-wen from Aberystwyth promenade (Day 9)*

The beach crossing of the Afon Cledan near Llansantffraid on Day 11 can be difficult when the river is in spate: a short inland detour is available.

Between Tal-y-bont and Barmouth the official Wales Coast Path at present is actually along the main A496 for 4km (2½ miles), which is highly unsatisfactory. This guide gives an unofficial beach alternative (low tide only) and an unofficial and highly recommended hill alternative. For times of low tides useful websites are www.news.bbc.co.uk/weather/coastandsea and www.tidetimes.org.uk.

Other suggested alternatives, where the official route is unsatisfactory, are between Minffordd and Penrhyndeudraeth, south of Maentwrog, at Harlech, at Tre'r-ddôl, near Tywyn and at Machynlleth. A short off-route detour is also suggested at Furnace.

**Walking with dogs**
The path passes from time to time through areas with livestock, through areas important for wildlife and close to cliff edges, so if you must take a dog with you it must be kept under close control.

## WHEN TO GO

Given the unpredictability of the British weather these days, there is no guarantee that you will enjoy more favourable conditions at certain times of the year, although on average the months of April to July are the driest (or should that be least wet?). Often, however, the coastal strip will be pleasant while the weather just inland is poor. From spring into summer, when the wildflowers are at their best, is also a good time to be walking the path. Some people may prefer early autumn, when the trees are just starting to turn. And while

*For a short time the path follows the pebble beach south of Llanrhystud (Day 11)*

*(left) The buzzard is the symbol for the Ardudwy Way (Day 4; hill alternative); (upper right) A Ceredigion Coast Path waymarker; (lower right) A Wales Coast Path waymarker*

winter is unlikely to be a good time to be walking the whole path, a short section on a couple of well-chosen calm days would be rewarding if you are especially interested in the wintering birdlife on the marshes and in the estuaries.

In August – the high season for holidaymakers – accommodation in the main resorts can get booked up, so if this is your chosen time to walk the coast path it would be wise to book your accommodation well in advance.

## SIGNPOSTING AND WAYMARKING

The Wales Coast Path symbol is used between Porthmadog and Borth, while on the Ceredigion Coast Path the symbol generally used shows an outline of the headland of Ynys Lochtyn. On the whole the waymarking is good, but not foolproof; on complicated sections follow the route directions and the sketch maps closely.

## SAFETY

Coastal walking is a great experience, but be alert to the dangers. Coastal conditions can be highly variable and can change quickly. Take extra care in high winds and do not venture to the cliff edge. Remember the coast can be subject to erosion and cliff falls. Follow any diversions in place. Check tide times in advance where the walk goes along beaches that are covered at high tide; use the alternative routes as necessary and note any possible escape routes. In an emergency call 999. Once connected to the emergency operator, explain the situation so that the appropriate service (Coastguard, Ambulance or Police) can be alerted, but be aware that mobile phone coverage is patchy.

## MAPS

The following OS maps cover the route in this guide:

- Landranger: 124 (Porthmadog and Dollgellau); 135 (Aberystwyth and Machynlleth); 145 (Cardigan/Aberteifi and Mynydd Preseli); 146 (Lampeter and Llandovery/Llanbedr Pont Steffan a Llanymddyfri)
- Explorer: OL18 (Harlech, Porthmadog and Bala); OL23 (Cadair Idris and Bala Lake); 198 (Cardigan and New Quay); 199 (Lampeter); 213 (Aberystwyth and Cwm Rheidol)

The extracts from the Landranger maps in this guide show the terrain immediately adjacent to the path. For the wider context the relevant Explorer maps are highly recommended.

The sketch maps, at a scale of approximately 1:25,000, show complicated sections of the path in greater detail.

## GETTING THERE

By train there are reasonable services from London Euston via Birmingham; from Birmingham itself; from Manchester via Shrewsbury and from the north of England and Scotland via Wolverhampton. All these trains go via Machynlleth, where the train divides – one part going on to Porthmadog (then Pwllheli), the other to Aberystwyth.

By coach there are routes from London, Birmingham, Manchester and Glasgow to Pwllheli for onward trains to Porthmadog, and a long-distance bus links Cardiff with Aberystwyth via Aberaeron.

To drive to Porthmadog from London and the southeast, use the M1, M6 and M54, the A5 to Betws-y-coed, then the A470 and A487. From the Midlands and the east make for the A5, then follow the route as above. From the Manchester and Liverpool areas get on to the M56, then follow the A55 coast road to Bangor and the A487 via Caernarfon. From the north and northeast of England and from Scotland, either travel down the M6 to join the M56, or travel down the A1 and join the M56 via the M62 and M6. To pick up your car from the end of the walk you can use one of the regular buses from Cardigan to Aberystwyth, then the train via Dovey Junction or Machynlleth to Porthmadog.

To return home by public transport from the end of the walk at Cardigan, use one of the regular buses to Carmarthen for trains or National Express coaches to London, the Midlands and further north.

See Appendix C for website details and telephone numbers of travel organisations.

For those travelling by air, Manchester and Birmingham International Airports are the best

*A train leaves Tywyn on the Talyllyn Railway (Day 6)*

arrival points, both linked to the national rail network.

## GETTING AROUND

Public transport along the walk is generally quite good. Regular buses and trains link most of the settlements along the coast, making it possible, with careful planning, to use public transport either at the start or end of a day's walk.

Between New Quay and Cardigan, Ceredigion County Council's coastal Cardi Bach bus can collect and set you down at convenient locations within a defined zone, and can be booked in advance. For a time-table go to www.ceredigioncoastpath. org.uk/cardi-bach.html or telephone 0845 686 0242.

There are railway stations at Porthmadog, Minffordd, Penrhyndeudraeth, Llandecwyn*, Talsarnau*, Tygwyn*, Harlech, Llandanwg*, Pensarn*, Llanbedr*, Dyffryn Ardudwy*, Tal-y-bont*, Llanaber*, Barmouth, Morfa Mawddach*, Fairbourne, Llwyngwril*, Tonfanau*, Tywyn, Aberdyfi, Machynlleth, Dovey Junction, Borth and Aberystwyth.

The stations marked * are request stops.

## ACCOMMODATION

Appendix B lists places with accommodation (and type of accommodation available) at the time of writing, and Appendix C lists the tourist information centres relevant to the coast path. A useful website is www.visitwales.co.uk; for information specific to the Ceredigion Coast Path visit www.discoverceredigion.co.uk. An online search for hotels, guest houses and B&Bs in specific towns and villages is also a good way of finding somewhere to stay. For people who prefer to carry their accommodation on their backs, there are many official campsites (which are primarily caravan sites) along the coast; the list at Appendix B includes camping options. There are only two youth hostels convenient to the route in this guide: one at Borth and one at Poppit Sands (west of St Dogmaels).

### Cab-a-bag scheme: luggage transfer

A luggage transfer scheme operates along the Ceredigion Coast Path, enabling walkers to forward larger bags from one overnight stay to another and carry a light pack for the walk itself. See the 'Walking' section at www.discoverceredigion.co.uk for further details.

## WHAT TO TAKE

As some sections of the walk are quite rough and rocky, and those across fields can be muddy at times, hiking boots rather than trainers are recommended. Always carry suitable wet-weather clothing, including lightweight overtrousers for rainy days and for when the walk goes through wet vegetation. A compass is unlikely to be needed (except on

the hill alternative between Tal-y-bont and Barmouth) but do carry a charged mobile phone, noting that coverage can be very patchy. While there are frequent places offering refreshment, it is important to carry ample food and drink, especially in hot weather. And do not forget to take high factor sun cream.

## VISITOR ATTRACTIONS

You may wish to build an extra hour or so, or an extra day as appropriate, into your walking schedule to visit one or more of the following attractions (listed here in the order in which you will encounter them):

- Welsh Highland Railway, Porthmadog – runs from the end of March to the end of October www.festrail.co.uk
- Ffestiniog Railway, Porthmadog – runs from February to December www.festrail.co.uk
- Portmeirion tourist village – open all year from 9.30am–7.30pm www.portmeirion-village.com
- Harlech Castle – open March, April, May, June, September and October 9.30am–5.00pm; July and August 9.30am–6.00pm; November, December, January and February 10.00am–4.00pm (11.00am–4.00pm Sunday)
- Fairbourne Steam Railway – runs from the end of March to the end of October, with limited days in February www.fairbournerailway.com

*The eclectic mix of buildings at Portmeirion (Day 1)*

- Talyllyn Railway, Tywyn – runs from the end of March to the end of October, with limited days in February, November and December www.talyllyn.co.uk
- Owain Glyndŵr Centre, Machynlleth – open from March to the end of September 10.00am–5.00pm; and from October to the end of December 11.00am–4.00pm www.canolfanglyndwr.org
- Centre for Alternative Technology, Machynlleth – open seven days a week, from Easter to the end of October, 10.00am–5.00pm www.cat.org.uk. (There are regular buses from Machynlleth.)
- Ceredigion Museum, Aberystwyth – open Monday to Saturday, from April to September 10.00am–5.00pm; and from October to March 12 noon–4.30pm www.ceredigion.gov.uk
- Vale of Rheidol Railway, Aberystwyth – runs from April to the end of October, with limited service in February and March www.rheidolrailway.co.uk
- Dylan Thomas Trail, New Quay (see www.newquay-westwales.co.uk/trail)
- St Dogmaels Abbey, St Dogmaels – open all year 10.00am–4.00pm (11.00am–3.00pm Sunday). There is an adjoining Coach House museum and café.

## USING THIS GUIDE

The route is divided up into day walks, each ending at a place with accommodation. The suggested sections are not written in tablets of stone

*Bright seafront houses at Borth (Day 9)*

and, based on the information in the appendices, you may opt to cover shorter or longer distances.

For each day walk an information box gives details on the walk's start and finish points, length, amount of ascent and descent, overall time it might take, OS maps required, any opportunities for refreshments along the way, public transport and accommodation. Timings are based on the speed of a walker of average fitness, allowing for rest and refreshment stops and for the nature of the terrain. You will need to add in extra time should you wish to visit one or more of the attractions en route, such as Harlech Castle or a narrow gauge railway.

Each route includes extracts from the appropriate OS Landranger map. A number of sketch maps at a scale of approximately 1:25,000 are included

to show the route in more detail over complicated sections. The maps in the guide are not intended as a substitute for the overall OS maps themselves, which walkers should also take with them. The 1:25,000 Explorer maps are especially recommended.

In the route descriptions key features that appear on the OS and sketch maps are shown in **bold** type to help with navigation.

In the appendices you will find a summary of the route distances and ascents/descents, and information on facilities such as places with accommodation, shops, cash points and where you can find a place to have lunch or an evening meal, and finally the addresses, websites and telephone numbers of useful contacts, including tourist information centres.

# THE SNOWDONIA COAST PATH

## DAY 1
### *Porthmadog to Maentwrog*

| | |
|---|---|
| **Start** | Glaslyn Bridge, Porthmadog (SH 570 384) |
| **Finish** | St Twrog's Church, Maentwrog (SH 664 405) |
| **Distance** | 14.5km (9 miles) |
| **Ascent** | 325m (1065ft) |
| **Descent** | 290m (950ft) |
| **Time** | 5hrs |
| **Maps** | OS Landranger 124; OS Explorer OL18 |
| **Refreshments** | Wide choice at Porthmadog; pubs and café at Penrhyndeudraeth; Oakeley Arms at Tan-y-bwlch and pub at Maentwrog |
| **Public transport** | Regular buses from Porthmadog to Maentwrog and Pwllheli; trains to Pwllheli and all stations to Machynlleth and national routes |
| **Accommodation** | Porthmadog (B&Bs, guest houses, hotels, campsites); Minffordd (B&B); Portmeirion (hotels); Penrhyndeudraeth (B&B, campsite); Tan-y-bwlch (hotel); Maentwrog (B&B, hotel) |

The walk begins with a mixture of road, lanes and field paths to Penrhyndeudraeth. Thereafter it is mainly through forest on paths and forest roads, with many ups and downs and some complicated route-finding at times. The going is generally firm underfoot.

If time allows you may wish to arrive the day before the walk to enjoy a ride on either the Ffestiniog Railway or the Welsh Highland Railway. The walk leaves Porthmadog across The Cob in company with the Ffestiniog Railway before taking to the woods and fields on the headland above Portmeirion, with wide views opening up across the estuary of the Glaslyn. Consider taking quiet lanes rather than the official main road into Penrhyndeudraeth. The path then makes a long loop inland to the crossing point on the Dwyryd, at first through open country with great views ahead to

Moelwyn Bach and later through mixed forest, where route directions need to be followed closely. The Ffestiniog Railway is never far away. The route descends via lovely Llyn Mair to Tan-y-bwlch, with a short section of main road to Maentwrog.

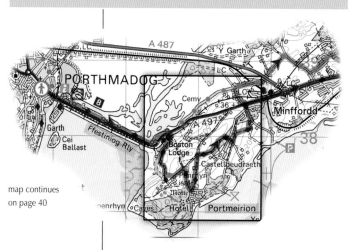

map continues
on page 40

If you are walking the **Wales Coast Path** in its entirety you will just have completed the Lleyn Peninsula Coast Path section from Caernarfon, a distance of some 145km (90 miles), over cliffs, moors, hills and beaches, following in the footsteps of the Bardsey pilgrims. See *The Lleyn Peninsula Coastal Path* (Cicerone: second edition, 2006), by John Cantrell.

The Snowdonia Coast Path starts where the Lleyn Peninsula Coast Path finishes, at the bridge over the Glaslyn. Leave **Porthmadog** past the terminus of the Welsh Highland and Ffestiniog Railways. Cross The Cob, either on the cycleway, the official route, or the right of way alongside the Ffestiniog Railway. ◀ On a good day there are splendid views north to Moel Ddu, Cnicht and the Moelwyns.

The right of way joins the cycleway at the far end of The Cob.

*Porthmadog's harbour marks the end of the Lleyn Peninsula Coastal Path and the start of the Snowdonia Coast Path*

## PORTHMADOG AND THE FFESTINIOG RAILWAY

The terminus of the Ffestiniog and Welsh Highland Railways, Porthmadog is a busy little town with a fine backdrop of hills. In the late 18th century, entrepreneur William Madocks bought up and reclaimed large tracts of land in the area after inheriting a sizeable sum of money from his father. Porthmadog began to grow, and Madocks' construction of the embankment (known as The Cob) began in 1808, with the official opening on 17 September 1811. The diverted Glaslyn now flowed past Porthmadog, creating a harbour for shipbuilding and slate export.

The Ffestiniog Railway, approved by an Act of Parliament in 1832 to bring slate down from Blaenau Ffestiniog, is the oldest independent railway in the world. Empty trucks were originally horse-drawn from Porthmadog up to Blaenau Ffestiniog, then the laden trucks, which also carried the horses, travelled back down with the aid of gravity. Steam was later introduced. The line closed in 1946, but it was partly reopened as a tourist attraction in 1954, eventually being restored all the way up to Blaenau.

The narrow gauge Welsh Highland Railway, between Caernarfon and Porthmadog, was fully reopened in 2011 after 50 years of hard work, public inquiries and much controversy. The railway had evolved over many decades, taking over the moribund Croesor Tramway and serving the slate quarries in Nant Gwynant. The line, never a commercial success, ran until 1937.

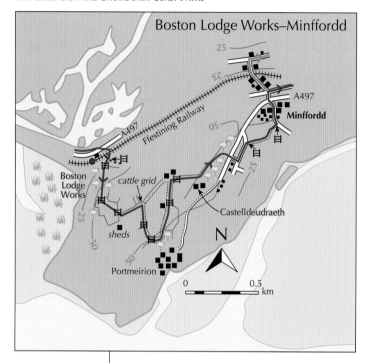

Boston Lodge Works–Minffordd

Ffestiniog Railway
A497
A497
**Minffordd**
Boston
Lodge
Works
*cattle grid*
Castelldeudraeth
*sheds*
N
Portmeirion
0          0.5
km

See Boston Lodge
Works–Minffordd
sketch map.

◀ Continue to a lay-by and cross the main road to head up a lane, then cross the railway near the **Boston Lodge Works**, keeping right at a fork. The narrow gauge engines and rolling stock are built and maintained at Boston Lodge Works. Continue through a wood and at its end enter a field (gate). Cross to a gate in the far top corner (by **sheds**) and continue on a track to a 'crossroads' near a **cattle grid**. Go right to follow the path down through trees, via a couple of gates, soon heading past the upper areas of **Portmeirion**. Continue leftwards via a field path to a further gate and along a lane to some buildings on either side of it.

Created in the 1920s, **Portmeirion**, the brainchild of architect Clough Williams-Ellis, is a bizarre collection of buildings salvaged from Britain and abroad. A Jacobean town hall stands cheek by jowl with an Italian campanile; Mediterranean-style houses are juxtaposed with a Buddha and cherubs. Distinguished visitors have included George Bernard Shaw and King Zog of Albania, and the 1960s cult TV series *The Prisoner* was set here. It is all whimsically entertaining but highly commercialised and busy.

Go right just before the buildings and continue along the field edge to a wide track through a wood. Cross the access road for Portmeirion (go right here if you wish to visit the village) and continue ahead on tarmac to a T-junction. Turn left here and, after 200 metres, go through the wicket gate on the right and continue around a field edge to reach a road at **Minffordd**. Turn left and follow the road to its junction with the A497. The official route follows the main road to **Penrhyndeudraeth**, turning left at the Griffin Hotel into the main shopping street.

*The lovely view back to Porthmadog and Moel-y-gest from above Boston Lodge Works*

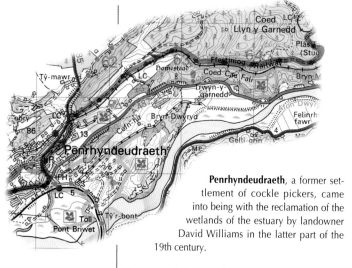

**Penrhyndeudraeth**, a former settlement of cockle pickers, came into being with the reclamation of the wetlands of the estuary by landowner David Williams in the latter part of the 19th century.

map continues on page 42

**Recommended alternative avoiding the A497**

Rather than follow the main road, it is more pleasant to cross it and walk down the lane over the Ffestiniog Railway to a T-junction, where you turn right. In a kilometre, after passing under the A487 and the Ffestiniog Railway, take the road on the left.

Where the road dips, ignore the right of way on the right and in another 100 metres, where a little road goes off to the left, turn right on a path between houses. (Anyone with a dog will need to continue along the road, bearing right to the centre of Penrhyndeudraeth.) Head through trees to a recreation ground, then go straight on at a junction and exit via a small car park to reach the main road in **Penrhyndeudraeth**. Go left.

Designated in 1951, Snowdonia is the second-largest of the national parks in England and Wales.

Set off along the side road by the main village car park. Where it bends right (in nearly a kilometre) go left up the lane and in 30 metres turn right to go up some steps. Pass under the Ffestiniog Railway to the main A4085, go right and immediately right again on a tarmac lane. The path has now entered Snowdonia National Park. ◀ Follow the

lane to its end at the house of Rhiw Goch, which is near the **level crossing** (LC) marked on the OS map. The prominent mountain ahead is Moelwyn Bach.

*A bright array of flags above shops in Penrhyndeudraeth*

> At 710m (2329ft) **Moelwyn Bach** is the second-highest peak (after Moelwyn Mawr) in the Moelwyn range, which extends from Porthmadog to Bwlch y Rhediad near Moel Siabod.

Pass left of the house and in 30 metres go half right on a path to a kissing gate. Wind through the woods parallel to the **Ffestiniog Railway**. Where the railway curves right, keep ahead and fork right after 50 metres. Drop to a footbridge over a stream (this is the Afon Cae-Fali). The path in the woods is not quite clear now for about 200 metres. Go up the bank, bear right and then very quickly left and up again: look out for a couple of steps. The path goes up several more steps, over an old wall, and turns sharp right and then quickly sharp left.

The path winds through the trees and soon drops steeply to come out above the Ffestiniog Railway, continuing as a wide terrace path. At a fork keep left (ahead),

back on a narrower path. Cross a footbridge at a small reservoir, walk over a rise and reach a wide stone track. Bear right.

Follow the path for about a kilometre, curving left (another track comes in from the right) to reach a fork. Head right and downhill, soon going over a level crossing, leaving the Ffestiniog Railway behind. Keep left at the wide track met at a bend and go down to **Llyn Mair**.

*Secluded Llyn Mair above Tan-y-bwlch*

**Llyn Mair** is an artificial lake, created, according to some sources, in 1886 by William Edward Oakeley of Plas Tan-y-bwlch as a 21st birthday present for his daughter Mary (*Mair* in Welsh),

although other sources claim the lake was created by Mary herself. Nowadays it provides a good habitat for winter wild ducks.

Bear right at a fork, continue down to the drive of Plas Tan-y-bwlch and go left to the B4410 near the Oakeley Arms.

The house of **Plas Tan-y-bwlch**, which had been held by the Oakeley family (managers of the lucrative Oakeley Slate Quarry) was acquired in 1969 by Merioneth County Council and in 1975 became a Snowdonia National Park environmental studies centre.

Go right to the main road and then turn left. Cross the old bridge over the Dwyryd in the Vale of Ffestiniog and continue ahead to **Maentwrog**.

The village of **Maentwrog** stands on the line of the Roman road of Sarn Helen. In legend, 'Twrog's stone' refers to the boulder hurled by giant Twrog onto the village to destroy a pagan altar. The earlier Welsh mythology of *The Mabinogion* mentions the name as the burial place of one Pryderi, killed at Glaslyn. The stone stands beside the church, dedicated to Twrog, a British saint whose life spanned the fifth and sixth centuries. The village grew a little in the 19th century to house workers in the nearby slate quarries.

# DAY 2
*Maentwrog to Harlech*

| | |
|---|---|
| **Start** | St Twrog's Church, Maentwrog (SH 664 405) |
| **Finish** | Harlech railway station (SH 580 313) |
| **Distance** | 18.5km (11½ miles) |
| **Ascent** | 395m (1295ft) |
| **Descent** | 410m (1345ft) |
| **Time** | 6hrs |
| **Maps** | OS Landranger 124; OS Explorer OL18 |
| **Refreshments** | Nothing until Harlech, then a reasonable choice |
| **Public transport** | Buses to Harlech, Porthmadog and Barmouth; trains from Harlech to Machynlleth and Pwllheli and all intermediate stations |
| **Accommodation** | Talsarnau (hotel); Harlech (B&Bs, guest houses, hotels, campsites) |

The first part of the walk is strenuous, with a couple of big climbs and some fiddly route-finding across enclosed land south of Maentwrog. The second part is mostly level on generally good tracks or field footpaths. A steep road-climb from Maentwrog leads to an area of small enclosures where route-finding needs concentration, but there are great views to the Moelwyns, Manod Mawr and the northern outliers of the Rhinogs. A quiet lane leads down to a crossing of the Afon Prysor, and this is followed by a steady climb through forest to lovely Llyn Tecwyn Uchaf.

A good path descends to the Glastraeth saltmarsh (close to the railway station of Llandecwyn). Following a flood bank there is a fine prospect across Traeth Bach to Portmeirion and Ynys Gifftan, and in clear weather to the mountains of Snowdonia. The path passes the tiny church at Ynys and leads between knolls to Morfa Harlech. The approach to Harlech is probably the least interesting stretch of the whole walk, being dead level, passing some huge recycling sheds and heading along a concrete lane and over flat fields.

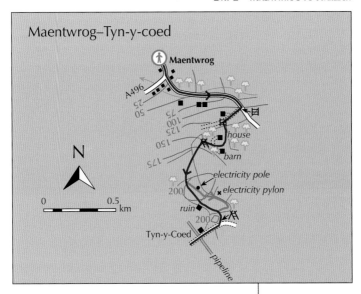

## Maentwrog–Tyn-y-coed

▶ Head south from St Twrog's Church for 100 metres, then leave **Maentwrog** on the road climbing left and continue to the very top of the hill. Go through a gate on the right where a wide path leads ahead. In 200 metres, at a plantation corner, go through a wicket gate on the left, then climb beside a fence and pass left of a **house**. Routefinding for the next kilometre is complicated: follow the maps and directions carefully. Go right over a little rise and drop to the right side of a stone **barn**. Keep right on a path, but as this bends right head up the bank on the left (through bracken on an earthy path) and then among trees to a stile. Go half left and then right and around a patch of bracken to a wall gap (muddy).

Now go half left in a rough field, keeping left of scattered trees, and pass through a wall gap. There are views ahead of the northern Rhinog

See Maentwrog–Tyn-y-Coed sketch map.

map continues on page 46

45

*Cloud caps the
Moelwyns above
Maentwrog*

hills of Moel Ysgyfarnogod, Diffwys and Moel y Gyrafolen.
The official route is difficult to follow for 500 metres as it
passes through areas of marsh, so it is recommended to go
forward instead to a wooden **electricity pole**, continue to
the next wall, cross it and bear left to an **electricity pylon**.
Bearing rightwards, follow a track down by a fence near
a plantation, curving right to reach and cross a stile. Now
back on the official route, go down to a road and turn right.

Follow the quiet road for nearly 2km (1¼ miles)
to the A496 by the former
**Maentwrog Power Station**.
Turn left across the river
(the Afon Prysor) and
left again through
a gate on a
wide path.

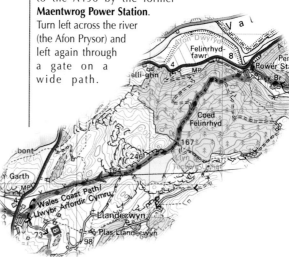

map continues
on page 49

Keep sharp right beyond a further gate and climb steeply through a wood. When you reach a forest road, bear right. In 1.5km go through a gate on the right-hand side at the edge of the forest (it is easily missed – the forest road is curving left) and follow a usually muddy path ahead.

This soon becomes a lovely path beside the reservoir of **Llyn Tecwyn Uchaf**. At the end of the reservoir continue down through gates and descend an excellent path with good views ahead (despite the electricity pylons) to Yr Eifl, Portmeirion and Ynys Gifftan. The path curves left at the foot of the hill and rises to pass behind a house before reaching a road. Turn right onto the **A496** and go straight over, just two kilometres from Penrhyndeudraeth!

### Changes to the path

Where the path crosses the A496 and the Pont Briwet toll road, major changes were in hand in 2014 comprising a new rail bridge, construction of a two-lane carriageway and new footpath and cycle path. The route of the coast path may be slightly affected. Keep a lookout for new signage. This scheme also enables a shortcut between Penrhyndeudraeth and Llandecwyn.

*A view back along the pleasant terrace path beside Llyn Tecwyn Uchaf*

Threatened with closure in the 1990s but happily retained, little Llandecwyn Station has the shortest of platforms, allowing access from only one door of any train.

For Llandecwyn Station keep ahead, otherwise bear left after 150 metres onto a tarmac lane. ◀ Pass in front of a cottage to a kissing gate and go left along the field edge below an old cliff line to a stile on the right. Cross the railway onto a flood embankment.

Follow alongside the saltmarsh of **Glastraeth** ('green beach') for 2.5km (1½ miles), past **Ynys Gifftan** ('Queen Anne's gift island', gifted by her in the early 18th century to Lord Harlech), with views across to Portmeirion. (Part way along at SH 608 363 a wide path goes off to the station and village of Talsarnau.)

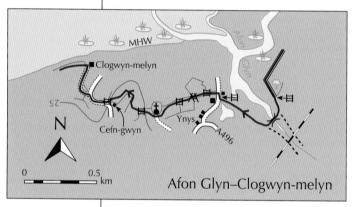

Afon Glyn–Clogwyn-melyn

See Afon Glyn–Clogwyn-melyn sketch map.

◀ Cross the **Afon Glyn** on a large footbridge over to the right and go right along the toe of the embankment to a road and the few houses at **Ynys**. If the day is fine there are wide views to the mountains: Moel Hebog, Snowdon, Cnicht and the northern Rhinogs especially. Go right then turn left in a few metres up a walled grassy path into a field. Walk up its left side to a stile, then follow the right side of the next two fields and pass left of the wall at **Ynys Church**.

Up until the Middle Ages, before the coastal flats and saltmarshes developed between the Dwyryd and Harlech, **Ynys Church** stood on an island,

accessible across the sands or by boat at high tides. The little church of Llanfihangel y Trethau (St Michael on the Beaches), embowered by yew trees and usually locked, dates mainly from 1871, although its foundations go back to the time of Owain Gwynedd, who reigned from 1131 to 1170. Inside, the splendid east window depicts Christ in Majesty with St Michael and Angels, in memory of Robert Jones-Morris, organist for 70 years until 1958. The window in the choir was designed and made by artist Polly Hope.

*A footbridge over the Afon Glyn affords excellent views of the Snowdonian mountains*

map continues
on page 51

*The ancient stone in the churchyard at Ynys*

In the graveyard, near the porch, stands a rough-hewn upright stone that bears a 12th-century inscription: 'Here is the grave of Wleder, mother of Hoedliw, who first built the church in the reign of King Owain Gwynedd'. Many of the gravestones are those of seafarers.

Cross the church access road and keep right. Cross a dip (steps) to a kissing gate, then go up through bracken to a crossing path. Follow this to the right and then follow the wall towards buildings (**Cefn-gwyn**). Keep to their right, pass through a kissing gate and continue onto a lane. Go right, and in 150 metres fork left to reach a house (**Clogwyn-melyn**). Find the rather hidden start of a footpath on the left and follow it through bracken.

At a kissing gate head across the grassy swathe, keeping left of a knoll until you reach a further kissing gate in 500 metres. Keep along the toe of the knoll on the left to reach another kissing gate at a house (**Glan-y-morfa**) on the edge of Morfa Harlech National Nature Reserve. Pass in front of the house to another kissing gate and turn left on a wide track. Fork right into the farmyard of **Glan-y-mor**, and just before the end of the main building go left through yet another kissing gate on the left (hidden by a wall) and continue into a field.

> The huge **Morfa Harlech National Nature Reserve** extends from the Glaslyn and Dwyryd estuaries to Traeth Bach and the sand dunes west of Harlech. The saltmarshes and mudflats are important winter feeding grounds for a wide variety of birds, and the Harlech dunes are one of the finest dune systems in Britain.

Cross diagonally to a large metal gate. Cross the next pasture (bullocks may be grazing here) to the far corner by a pine wood (kissing gate). The next kilometre is probably the least pleasant of the

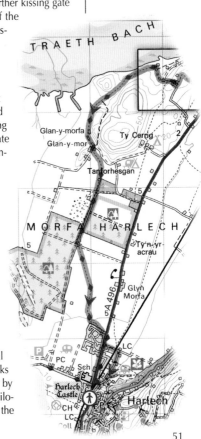

51

*A spectacular example of medieval architecture, Harlech Castle seems a natural extension of the rock spur upon which it was built*

whole walk! Go along a field edge, cross the access road to large recycling sheds (where an unwelcome smell might assail the nostrils) and continue along a straight concrete lane.

At a junction of lanes, go through a kissing gate on the left and head diagonally across the next two fields. **Harlech Castle** is now prominent up ahead. In the third field go diagonally over to the far side, then continue along a fence to a footbridge and cross into a willow copse. Follow the winding path to arrive alongside houses. The official route goes through a kissing gate on the right, then between houses to a road, left to the main A496 and right into **Harlech**.

### Recommended alternative into Harlech

Before reaching the main road, keep right on the parallel estate road to its exit (onto the main road). Cross half right and go down a path, soon crossing over the railway, and go right along a quiet road leading to **Harlech Station** in 600 metres. Cross the level crossing, go left on the main road and in 25 metres turn right on a road signed for the beach.

## HARLECH

On rising land above the coastal flats, Harlech is dominated by its fine castle, situated to command views over the sweep of Cardigan Bay and the hills of Snowdonia, with the sea once lapping the base of its rocky bluff before the dunes developed.

It is this high vantage point that features in *The Mabinogion* (medieval stories), in the tale of Branwen, daughter of Llŷr. The 19th-century translation tells us that it is from 'Harddlech' (as the town's name was spelt at that time) that Branwen's brother Bendigeidfran spies the ships of Matholwch, King of Ireland, approaching. Branwen departs to marry the king, and much later their son, Gwern, is killed in a war between Wales and Ireland. Beside the castle stands Ivor Roberts-Jones' dramatic sculpture depicting Bendigeidfran carrying back the body of Gwern.

Early sources suggest the name Harlech derives from *ardd* (high) and *llech* (rock), while later sources favour *hardd* (fair) and *llech*.

The castle, the construction of which began in 1283, is one of Edward I's 'iron ring of castles'. In 1404 it was taken by Owain Glyndŵr, becoming his official residence, until 1409 saw its recapture by Harry of Monmouth, the future Henry V. From 1461 to 1468 the future Henry VII held out against a siege by Yorkists, before the castle was taken, the surrender commemorated in the song *Men of Harlech*. The castle fell into disrepair, but was rebuilt during the Civil War for the king. In 1647 it became the last castle to fall to parliamentary forces. The upper town in the vicinity of the castle is attractive, perhaps less so the areas along the main road.

# DAY 3
## Harlech to Tal-y-bont

| | |
|---|---|
| **Start** | Harlech railway station (SH 580 313) |
| **Finish** | Footbridge over the Afon Ysgethin, Tal-y-bont (SH 589 218) |
| **Distance** | 17.25km (10¾ miles) |
| **Ascent** | 145m (475ft) |
| **Descent** | 120m (395ft) |
| **Time** | 5hrs |
| **Maps** | OS Landranger 124; OS Explorer OL18 |
| **Refreshments** | Seasonal café at Llandanwg; pubs at Llanbedr (600 metres off-route) and Tal-y-bont |
| **Public transport** | Buses to Maentwrog; trains to Machynlleth and Pwllheli and all intermediate stations |
| **Accommodation** | Llanfair and Llandanwg (B&Bs, campsite); Llanbedr (guest house, hotel, campsites); Shell Island (campsite); Tal-y-bont (B&B, campsites) |

This is a walk of generally easy gradients, with long sandy beaches, road, wide tracks and field footpaths to follow. Route-finding is straightforward apart from the very complex approach to Tal-y-bont.

If possible, time should be found to visit Harlech's castle before setting off. Soon after leaving Harlech, the sea proper (rather than estuary) is met for the first time. A fine stretch of sandy beach leads to a road walk down to Llandanwg with its tiny church hidden among the dunes. The way goes alongside the creek of Pensarn Harbour, with the big hill of Moelfre rising ahead. In company for a short while with the Afon Artro, the route reaches a road near Llanbedr and follows a well-surfaced path heading out across the saltmarsh to the campsite of Shell Island – and a magnificent sweep of beach. A complicated route through small fields brings you to the lowest crossing point on the Ysgethin at Tal-y-bont.

Leave **Harlech** on the road near the station, signed to the beach. When you reach the sea on the path from the road end, head left along the beach for 2km (1¼ miles) to

*There is a fine view back over Morfa Harlech from the path at Llanfair*

some upward steps (where boulders begin). Cross the railway and zigzag up the cliff (the only coastal cliff on the whole of the path between Porthmadog and Borth). There is a sweeping view across the dunes with Snowdonia's mountains forming a backdrop in clear weather. Follow the main road rightwards at **Llanfair** and then go right on the Llandanwg road. As the road bends right at the end go forward on a tarmac lane, but first continue through the car park (café) to visit **Llandanwg church**.

At the southern end of Llandanwg, set among the dunes, is the little **church of St Tanwg**. Although the church dates to medieval times (13th century), it is thought that the site

map continues on page 57

has been used for worship since the fifth century, and it features two sixth-century inscribed stones.

Leave the lane at a kissing gate and go alongside a drainage ditch. You soon go across a channel and then along an embankment overlooking Pensarn Harbour. Immediately before the railway, cross a footbridge and take a curving line across the saltmarsh to the buildings of Pensarn Harbour and a wicket gate. Pass between the buildings to a level crossing by **Pensarn Station**.

Turn right on the main road (on a verge and then a parallel path) then cross a field to a footbridge over the Afon Artro. Follow its bank until you reach a road via a car park. Turn left for Llanbedr, otherwise go right on a path that runs parallel to the road.

*The Rhinog ridge and the dome of Moelfre rise above Pensarn Harbour*

The coastal plain village of **Llanbedr** originally grew around the slate industry. The nearby Royal Aerospace Establishment came into being in the Second World War as an airfield for day operations against enemy raiders.

Over the level crossing, follow the road past the derelict buildings of the former aerospace establishment (a poor section). Just before the beach, leave the road and turn left through a kissing gate on a straight path. The path runs at first across saltmarsh, then through reed beds, and finally through scrub woodland to arrive at a wide track on the edge of the Shell Island campsite.

*The path heads across levels to Shell Island*

When in the early 19th century the Earl of Winchelsea diverted the River Artro to add reclaimed land to his estates, the old channel became covered in extensive dunes. At 180ha (445 acres) **Shell Island** is the site of one of the largest tented campsites in Europe.

map continues on page 58

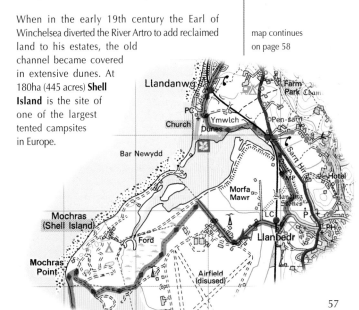

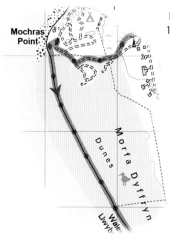

Bearing right, follow this vehicle track for 1.5km through the campsite and areas of dunes, gradually curving north to a junction of several campsite roads. Go sharp left up to, and through, a rough car park and down onto the long beach at **Mochras Point**.

Running out to sea from Mochras Point is **St Patrick's Causeway**, the most northerly and the longest of a number of shingle banks (sarnau) in the north of Cardigan Bay. This glacial moraine feature, left when ice retreated at the end of the last Ice Age, runs for some 20km (12½ miles) and is visible at very low tides. It is one of the banks said to protect the legendary drowned land of Cantref-y-Gwaelod, stretching 30km (18½ miles) west of today's coastline: a kingdom lost when Seithenyn, a drunken watchman (or in some versions a prince of the realm), failed to warn of an approaching storm, which broke through the floodgates at Sarn Badrig.

Near Tywyn is the smaller bank of Sarn y Bwlch, and the shingle spit of Sarn Gynfelyn can be seen from the coast path further south at Wallog.

Follow the beach for 4km (2½ miles) alongside the dunes of **Morfa Dyffryn**, passing through a section of about a kilometre that is designated as a naturist beach.

**Morfa Dyffryn** is a National Nature Reserve with a dynamic dune system supporting a range of important plants and animals. Naturism has been practised on the beach since the 1930s; the designated section can get quite busy on fine summer days.

Leave the beach (in this section known as Bennar Beach) at a tall red-and-white post, SH 569 225. This is just west of the picnic table symbol on the OS map.

map continues on page 60

*Moelfre (centre) and Rhinog Fawr (left) are seen as the path leaves Bennar Beach*

(The substantial Afon Ysgethin, which outflows to the sea just to the south, is a barrier to further progress along the beach.) Follow a boardwalk inland to a road and head along this, enjoying lovely views ahead (in fair weather) of Rhinog Fawr, the rounded hill of Moelfre, and Diffwys and Llawlech.

▶ Just before the buildings of **Bennar Fawr** at **Bennar**, go through a wicket gate on the right. From here

See Bennar Fawr–Tal-y-bont sketch map.

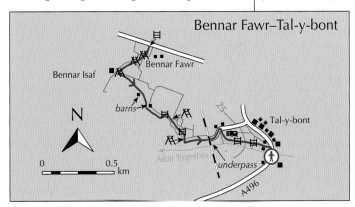

Bennar Fawr–Tal-y-bont

Bennar Isaf

Bennar Fawr

barns

N

Afon Ysgethin

Tal-y-bont

underpass

A496

0        0.5
         km

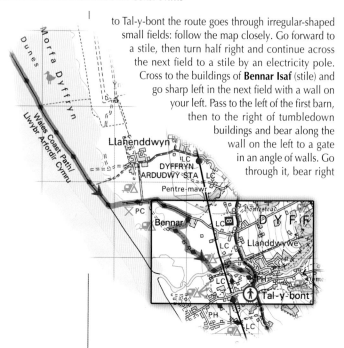

to Tal-y-bont the route goes through irregular-shaped small fields: follow the map closely. Go forward to a stile, then turn half right and continue across the next field to a stile by an electricity pole. Cross to the buildings of **Bennar Isaf** (stile) and go sharp left in the next field with a wall on your left. Pass to the left of the first barn, then to the right of tumbledown buildings and bear along the wall on the left to a gate in an angle of walls. Go through it, bear right

The whole area around Tal-y-bont is strewn with signs of ancient settlement, especially cairns, stone circles and burial chambers, a number of which are seen on the hill alternative described in Day 4.

and veer away from the wall to a stile in the wall ahead. Once through the gate at the end of an irregular field, follow the wall on the right in the field beyond to a corner stile. Go forward then turn left on a track and pass underneath the railway.

Bear left on the lane, pass a farm and enter a **caravan site** by its reception building on the right. Curve left with the tarmac drive to reach a gate. Go up the next (camping) field to a wicket gate near the top and continue forward past chalets to reach the main A496 in **Tal-y-bont**. Turn right to reach the footbridge over the Afon Ysgethin. ◄

# DAY 4
*Tal-y-bont to Barmouth*

| | |
|---|---|
| **Start** | Footbridge over the Afon Ysgethin, Tal-y-bont (SH 589 218) |
| **Finish** | Barmouth Harbour (SH 615 155) |
| **Distance** | 8km (5 miles); beach alternative: 8.5km (5¼ miles); hill alternative: 14km (8¾ miles) |
| **Ascent** | 35m (115ft); beach alternative: 10m (30ft); hill alternative: 545m (1790ft) |
| **Descent** | 85m (280ft); beach alternative: 20m (65ft); hill alternative: 530m (1740ft) |
| **Time** | 2½hrs; hill alternative: 5hrs |
| **Maps** | OS Landranger 124; OS Explorer OL18, OL23 |
| **Refreshments** | Pub mid-way along main road section on official route (nothing on hill alternative); wide choice of cafés, pubs and restaurants in Barmouth |
| **Public transport** | Regular trains from Tal-y-bont and Barmouth to Porthmadog, Machynlleth and intermediate stations; buses link Harlech and Barmouth via Tal-y-bont and Llanaber |
| **Accommodation** | Barmouth (B&Bs, guest houses, hotels, campsites) |

At Tal-y-bont a decision must be made as to which route to follow to Barmouth. The official route crosses fields for a kilometre followed by a long 4km (2½ mile) slog on a main road: a poor option, even if there is a pavement all the way. There are also fiddly paths on the official route, partly through caravan parks. At low tide the long sandy beach could be followed, but **first check the tide times** as the beach is impassable in the vicinity of Llanaber at most states of the tide. In reasonable weather an unofficial hill alternative is highly recommended: it is well inland but follows good paths along part of the Ardudwy Way. Alternatively there are trains and buses from Tal-y-bont to Llanaber.

Unless you choose the more lengthy hill alternative, the official route and the beach alternative (low tide only) both make for a very short day. Either of the latter two options could therefore easily be tacked onto the previous or next day's walk.

The hill alternative is a fairly strenuous route, albeit with few steep gradients, that follows the waymarked Ardudwy Way for most of the day and begins with a beautiful climb through woods beside the Afon Ysgethin. A good path heads across the moorland beyond, which is easy to follow even in mist. The path reaches a dip in the southern Rhinogs ridge. In mist you may need a compass for the first kilometre of the route down the hillside beyond, but it is otherwise fairly well waymarked. The super-fit may keep to the ridge, with a wall as a sure guide. There are superb views throughout (not least towards Cadair Idris) and several antiquities along the way to add interest to a fine walk. If time and fitness allow, choose this alternative instead of the other routes.

All three options end with a walk along Barmouth's long promenade. (Self-respecting walkers will, of course, pass up the opportunity of a ride to the far end on the seasonal promenade road train.)

See Tal-y-bont–A496 sketch map.

**See page 64 for the hill alternative route description.**

◀ Cross the footbridge over the Afon Ysgethin in **Tal-y-bont** then turn sharp right on a footpath by the river. After two fields you reach a wicket gate where you turn left onto a lane. Bear right at a junction on a grassy path that leads to a **level crossing**. Cross to a kissing gate and head half right to a wicket gate and into a caravan

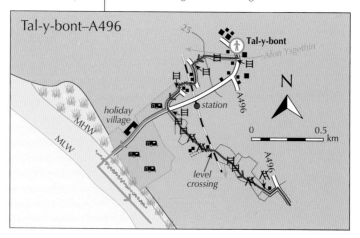

site. Continue ahead to some buildings and pass the site reception on your right. Follow a walled lane through the caravan site to a road and go right. From this point you may follow either the official route or, at low tide, the beach alternative.

*The Wales Coast Path goes through the popular coastal village of Tal-y-bont*

For the official route go immediately left (kissing gate) along the right side of a field, and in the next field go ahead to a facing gate. Continue forward to a stile by a barn and ahead between a wall (left) and buildings (right). Go left, then right at the entrance to the Sea Nymph Caravan Park and onward to a **level crossing**. Cross a little stream and pass rightwards through a gate. Continue through the succeeding fields via a kissing gate and stile and aim towards a house. Cross a stile into the garden and go up the drive to the main road. Follow it to the right and endure 4km (2½ miles) of main road walking.

At **Llanaber**, 500 metres after passing a cemetery, leave the road at SH 603 174 (by a coast path sign). Go down to a level crossing and join Barmouth Promenade.

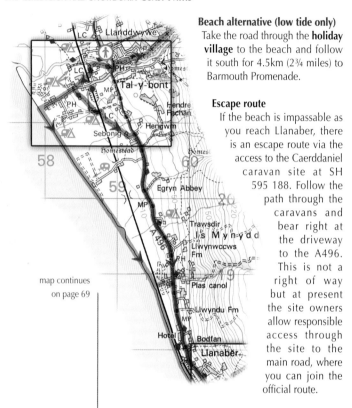

map continues
on page 69

### Beach alternative (low tide only)

Take the road through the **holiday village** to the beach and follow it south for 4.5km (2¾ miles) to Barmouth Promenade.

### Escape route

If the beach is impassable as you reach Llanaber, there is an escape route via the access to the Caerddaniel caravan site at SH 595 188. Follow the path through the caravans and bear right at the driveway to the A496. This is not a right of way but at present the site owners allow responsible access through the site to the main road, where you can join the official route.

The Ardudwy Way is a 40km (25-mile) trail from Llandecwyn to Barmouth, waymarked with a yellow buzzard symbol.

### Hill alternative

Immediately before the bridge over the Ysgethin in **Tal-y-bont**, turn left up a path signed as part of the Ardudwy Way. ◀ Pass immediately alongside the **Ysgethin Inn** (a former 19th-century woollen mill) and to the right of a stone building, thereafter following a lovely path up through the woods, parallel to the tumbling river, all the way (2km/1¼ miles) to a lane by a house. Bear right on the lane, passing over attractive **Pont Fadog** to its end at a gate.

Continue up a grassy track, keeping right at a fork. The way to the Bwlch y Rhiwgyr, on an old drovers road, is clear, much of it being alongside a wall. The gradients are easy until a final steepening to a gate at the pass.

*The Afon Ysgethin tumbles down through beautiful woodland*

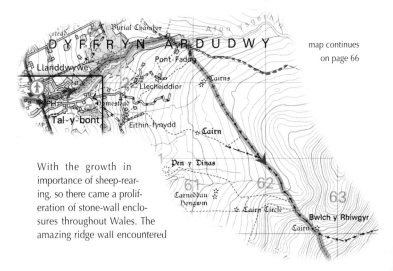

map continues on page 66

With the growth in importance of sheep-rearing, so there came a proliferation of stone-wall enclosures throughout Wales. The amazing ridge wall encountered

*Cadair Idris comes into view at Bwlch y Rhiwgyr*

at **Bwlch y Rhiwgyr** (the pass of the drovers) runs for an incredible 10km (6¼ miles) from the hill above Barmouth to the shoulder of Rhinog Fach. A ruined ring cairn at the pass was robbed for stone for the wall.

map continues on page 69

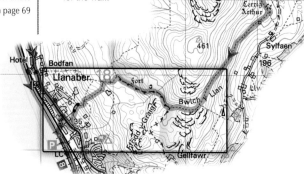

Go through the gate, turn right and head downhill. (A more strenuous option is to turn southwest up alongside the ridge wall, with the wall on your right, following the ridge and rejoining the described route near the Bwlch y Llan.) Follow the Ardudwy Way waymarkers to a gate and then a facing stile (encountering one or two small boggy patches and streamlets). With marvellous views over the Mawddach to Cadair Idris, continue to slant down the hillside and go through a gap in the wall on the left. Keep the wall now roughly on the right, and 1.3km after leaving the Bwlch y Rhiwgyr you arrive at **Cerrig Arthur**, referred to as an ancient stone circle but in reality just three upright stones.

Pass through a gate on the right and follow the path, climbing gradually via a gate and two stiles to a shallow pass, the **Bwlch y Llan**.

▶ The hill alternative path trends more westerly than that of the Ardudwy Way, which soon heads off to the left. Leave the Ardudwy Way and keep ahead, going northwest to a stile. Beyond this, at the top of an old

See Bwlch y Llan–A496 sketch map.

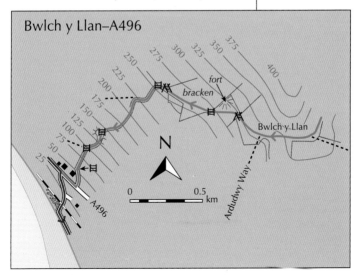

Bwlch y Llan–A496

*The view down the coast from the old fort near Bwlch y Llan*

inclined plane, bear half right and zigzag down below the rocky knoll of an ancient **fort** to reach a gate. At the far end of the next enclosure cross the stile and at once go through the gate on the left.

Descend between walls on a grassy path (which gets steeper and rougher lower down) to a wicket gate. Beyond the gate follow the right-hand wall downwards, bearing right to another wicket gate on the left. A walled path leads down to the back of some houses and then goes left to the A496 at **Llanaber**. Walk right for 200 metres and go down the lane with a coast path sign. Continue over the level crossing and join Barmouth Promenade.

**Note** At the time of going to press in early 2014, a temporary diversion is in place at Barmouth north promenade due to winter storm damage. See **www. walescoastpath. gov.uk** and click on *WCP Temporary Diversions*.

All three routes now follow Barmouth Promenade all the way to its far southern end, to finish the day's walk at **Barmouth Harbour**.

The old port at **Barmouth** lies tightly packed below steep cliffs and hillside, but behind the long promenade the more recent, rather poor development and tacky beach amusements are less appealing. From the Welsh *Abermawddach* (the mouth of the Mawddach), the town became 'Abermaw', which changed to 'Bermo' and finally mutated to 'Barmouth'. Trade in woollen cloth and the building of slate-trading boats were at one time the mainstays of the Barmouth economy. As they declined so Barmouth grew in popularity as a holiday resort.

Look out for Ty Gwyn Museum, a medieval townhouse dating back to 1460, built by Gruffydd Fychan. Here Henry VII's uncle, Jasper Tudor, is said to have plotted Richard III's downfall. Note also Ty Crwn Roundhouse of 1834, a lockup for drunks, in use until 1861 (one side for men, one for women).

*Rising steeply above Barmouth Harbour, the hill of Y Garn is the final height on the long Rhinog ridge*

69

From the road high above Friog there is a huge view back along the coast, here seen with cloud streaming off the hills

# DAY 5
## Barmouth to Llwyngwril

| | |
|---|---|
| **Start** | Barmouth Harbour (SH 615 155) |
| **Finish** | St Celynnin's Church, Llwyngwril (SH 591 095) |
| **Distance** | 13.75km (8¾ miles) |
| **Ascent** | 355m (1165ft) |
| **Descent** | 340m (1110ft) |
| **Time** | 5hrs |
| **Maps** | OS Landranger 124; OS Explorer OL23 |
| **Refreshments** | Café and pub in Fairbourne; pub in Llwyngwril |
| **Public transport** | Trains from Barmouth, Morfa Mawddach and Llwyngwril to Porthmadog and Machynlleth (continuing on the national rail network); buses link Fairbourne, Friog and Llwyngwril with Tywyn and Dolgellau |
| **Accommodation** | Fairbourne (B&B, guest house, hotel, campsites); Llwyngwril (B&Bs, guest houses, campsite) |

This fairly short day would enable you to include a ride on the Fairbourne Steam Railway. Via the long Barmouth Bridge the path crosses the Mawddach, backed by the Cadair Idris massif. There are pleasant views over to Barmouth as the path winds along the flood bank from Morfa Mawddach to the quiet seaside resort of Fairbourne, where it runs alongside the steam railway. There is a steep climb past the old Friog Slate Quarry, followed by a generally juicy path leading through a plantation and across a couple of streams. The way now follows a high moorland road (virtually traffic-free) passing several antiquities and commanding wonderful views along the coast. The section ends with an easy walk down to the pleasant village of Llwyngwril.

Walk along the quayside at **Barmouth Harbour** and continue under the railway, then turn right on the main road and continue for 350 metres. Drop down the path on the right and cross **Barmouth Bridge** (small toll).

*Barmouth Bridge takes the coast path across the Mawddach*

Opened in 1867, **Barmouth Bridge** remains the longest bridge in Wales at 700 metres long. There are 113 separate timber spans and 500 timber piles, with each support sunk 36m. In 1980 the bridge was closed due to shipworm damage, and was later saved through treatment with glass-reinforced cement.

At the far end cross the railway (level crossing) at **Morfa Mawddach Station** and follow the path along the embankment beside the estuary. ◀

Until 1960 Morfa Mawddach Station was Barmouth Junction Station, where the old line from Dolgellau met the extant Cambrian coast line. The station had five platforms!

When you reach the road at **Fairbourne** follow the path parallel to the sea wall, beside the narrow gauge railway, soon heading inland. Continue over the main line level crossing to the A493 at **Friog** and turn right.

The small resort of **Fairbourne** developed in the late 19th century on part of the estate belonging to the chairman of McDougalls Flour. A small narrow gauge steam railway, originally horse-drawn, was used to carry materials for the building of the village. Today it links the settlement with the end of

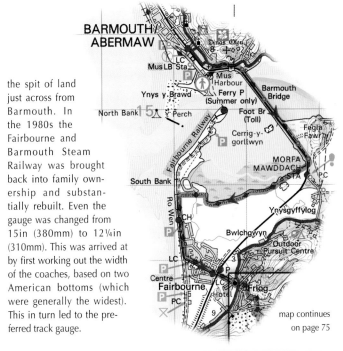

the spit of land just across from Barmouth. In the 1980s the Fairbourne and Barmouth Steam Railway was brought back into family ownership and substantially rebuilt. Even the gauge was changed from 15in (380mm) to 12¼in (310mm). This was arrived at by first working out the width of the coaches, based on two American bottoms (which were generally the widest). This in turn led to the preferred track gauge.

map continues on page 75

*Locomotive 'Sherpa' chugs along beside the coast path at Fairbourne*

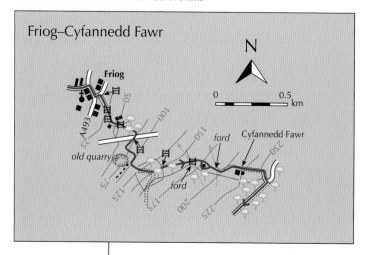

Friog–Cyfannedd Fawr

See Friog–Cyfannedd
Fawr sketch map.

◀ Almost at once turn left up Ffordd yr Esgob and go through the gate on the right in 40 metres via another kissing gate. Climb steeply to reach buildings, bearing left to a wicket gate and heading past a barn to reach a further wicket gate on the right. Follow a pleasant path through trees and then descend to a road. Go right and

*One of the standing stones beside the path near Cyfannedd Fawr*

in 25 metres turn left up an **old quarry** track, forking left as the spoil mounds of the disused Friog Slate Quarry are reached. Look out for a kissing gate off to the left in trees (easily missed). Beyond the gate, follow a path through the trees, ford a stream at a kissing gate and at a fork in grass take either path. Pass a stone building and walk up beside a wall, soon approaching the house of **Cyfannedd Fawr**. Follow its access drive to a road and turn right.

Follow the road through a plantation to open hill country, passing a couple of **standing stones** and, later, various other antiquities. Wide views open up along the coast and across to the Rhinogs. In about 2.5km (1½ miles), near a couple of ponds, leave the road by a track off to the left. Cross fields on an obvious path then go down a lane for a further kilometre to the main road in **Llwyngwril**, where you go left to reach St Celynnin's Church.

A number of ancient standing stones in the **Llwyngwril** area reputedly date from the time when the lowland giant Gwril and the giant Idris on Cadair Idris would hurl rocks at each other. Llwyngwril was a Quaker stronghold; there is a Quaker burial ground near the beach.

75

# DAY 6
## Llwyngwril to Aberdyfi

| | |
|---|---|
| **Start** | St Celynnin's Church, Llwyngwril (SH 591 095) |
| **Finish** | Aberdyfi seafront (SN 613 959) |
| **Distance** | 20km (12½ miles) |
| **Ascent** | 355m (1165ft) |
| **Descent** | 365m (1200ft) |
| **Time** | 6½hrs |
| **Maps** | OS Landranger 124, 135; OS Explorer OL23 |
| **Refreshments** | Various eateries and pubs in Tywyn and Aberdyfi |
| **Public transport** | Trains from Llwyngwril, Tonfanau, Tywyn and Aberdyfi to Porthmadog and intermediate stations, and to Machynlleth (continuing on the national rail network); buses link Llwyngwril and Tywyn via Rhoslefain (A493), and Tywyn and Machynlleth via Aberdyfi and Pennal |
| **Accommodation** | Tywyn (B&Bs, guest houses, campsites); Aberdyfi (B&Bs, guest houses, hotels) |

A steep climb from Llwyngwril leads to three cross-country kilometres (1¾ miles) where a close eye must be kept on the route directions as the way lies mainly through a complex of fields, some of which can be muddy. The way forward is not always obvious. Beyond Rhoslefain the route is more straightforward, following the contour along the hill foot to the Tonfanau Quarry. The path crosses the mouth of the Dysynni near Broad Water and is level to Tywyn. The day ends with a walk along a magnificent beach, on firm sands, to Aberdyfi.

The walk could be split into two by finishing the first day at Tywyn. On the second day you could enjoy a trip on the Talyllyn Railway to Nant Gwernol and back before making the 6.5km (4-mile) walk later in the afternoon along the beach to Aberdyfi.

Turn up the road by St Celynnin's Church in **Llwyngwril** and climb steeply for nearly a kilometre, passing near the gorse-covered mound of the Iron Age fort of

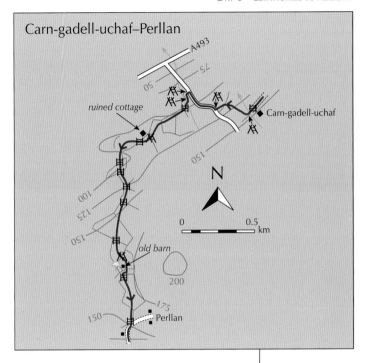

Carn-gadell-uchaf–Perllan

*ruined cottage*

Carn-gadell-uchaf

N

0    0.5
km

*old barn*

200

*Perllan*

**Castell y Gaer**, to the second of two cattle grids. Turn right along a concrete farm road to **Carn-gadell-uchaf**.

▸ Continue to a wicket gate beyond, then over a stream to a stile. Bear right in the field beyond, go through two wall gaps and turn left. Continue to a stile onto a road. Descend steeply for 400 metres then climb steps on the left to a stile. The next section is complicated and can get overgrown. In the field ignore the coast path sign by going right for a few metres, then curving left and heading uphill, parallel to a fence (tall bracken). Go up the side of a field for only a very short way. Look out for an easily missed waymarker 25 metres to the right. Force a way through the vegetation, cross a streamlet and reach a stile. Go forward and work a way left, parallel to

See Carn-gadell-uchaf–Perllan sketch map.

77

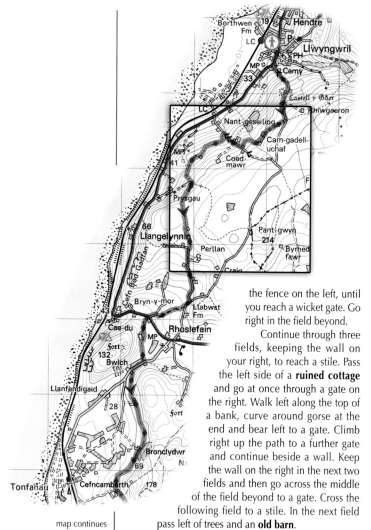

the fence on the left, until you reach a wicket gate. Go right in the field beyond.

Continue through three fields, keeping the wall on your right, to reach a stile. Pass the left side of a **ruined cottage** and go at once through a gate on the right. Walk left along the top of a bank, curve around gorse at the end and bear left to a gate. Climb right up the path to a further gate and continue beside a wall. Keep the wall on the right in the next two fields and then go across the middle of the field beyond to a gate. Cross the following field to a stile. In the next field pass left of trees and an **old barn**.

Enter the next field across a grassy 'lane', go to the far end and continue forward in the next field to a lane

map continues on page 82

near **Perllan**. Follow it down; it soon becomes tarmac-surfaced. After a sharp right bend go right (gate) down a hedged path that can be very muddy (use the adjoining field if necessary). At the A493 at **Rhoslefain** cross over and head up the farm lane to a gate on the left. ▶ Pass left of the buildings of Bron-y-foel and go across the next field. Aim towards the house seen ahead to reach a wicket gate (boggy ground). Cross a streamlet to a very wet path that leads up to a road by the house, where you go right.

Branch off left on a path before the next house and follow it to the buildings of Tyddyn Meurig (SH 571 049). Pass in front of the house then left of a barn and head up to a wicket gate. Follow the path parallel to the boundary on the right, heading past **Bronclydwr**.

Adjoining the historic farmhouse of **Bronclydwr** is an extensive plantsman's garden with a varied collection of plants, shrubs and trees, many of them rare and tender. The garden is currently open to the public one day a year as part of the National Gardens Scheme.

*The sea is glimpsed from the path near Rhoslefain*

The Rhoslefain area was once infamous for salt smuggling.

79

*The path descends on this wide track through the Tonfanau Quarry*

Continue to the Grade II listed buildings of **Cefncamberth**. Pass between buildings to a fork in the grassy path and keep forward (not left) through hydrangeas on a garden path to reach a wicket gate. Follow the boundary on the right to a further wicket gate and scramble up to emerge at the spoil of Tonfanau Quarry. Keep the spoil on your left and join a wide quarry road. Descend with it through the quarry (it is the coast path!) to a gate right of a large grey shed, and emerge onto a road. Keep a sharp lookout for lorries.

The largely worked-out **Tonfanau Quarry** comprises felsic tuff, an igneous rock formed 495 to 443 million years ago from explosive eruptions of silica-rich viscous magma, intruded into the much older Cambrian rocks.

Go right, and in just under a kilometre (300 metres short of lonely Tonfanau Station) go left on a metalled lane.

**Tonfanau** today consists of just a few farms and other buildings. It was the site of a Royal Artillery army base, set up in the Second World War, specialising in anti-aircraft training. The range and the Royal Electrical and Mechanical Engineers (REME) workshop lay between the railway and the sea, while the camp (where there are nowadays fields and blocks of woodland) lay east of the railway. Although it was closed in 1966, in 1972 it was briefly re-used as a refugee camp for over 1000 Ugandan Asians fleeing the regime of Idi Amin.

Tonfanau Station, which served the camp, is one of the quietest of railway stations. In the 1990s, after British Rail's attempt to close it was refused, it was upgraded, with lighting nowadays powered by its own wind turbine.

In 700 metres reach the Pont Tonfanau footbridge over the Dysynni, midway between **Broad Water** and the sea.

The fine **footbridge** over the Dysynni was installed in 2013, replacing a long-gone bailey bridge, so avoiding a lengthy inland detour via Bryncrug.

*The elegant Pont Tonfanau between Tonfanau and Tywyn*

Before the original road bridge fell into disrepair, this was the main A road north from Tywyn. Inland can be glimpsed the wide tidal lagoon of Broad Water. In the 18th and 19th centuries the lagoon was used for shipbuilding, predominantly of small ships to carry peat from the nearby peat bogs. Silting up put an end to this trade and the area is now a designated Site of Special Scientific Interest (SSSI), important for its many wetland birds.

Beyond the footbridge, the official route follows a road alongside the railway for 2km (1¼ miles) to a road junction, but it is a poor route.

### Recommended alternative avoiding the road

Cross the coastal flats as follows: 100 metres down the road turn through the gate on the left. Keep roughly parallel to the wooden electricity poles

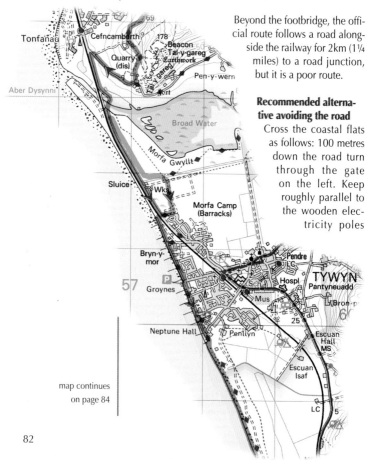

map continues on page 84

across the levels on a grassy path (do not attempt to find the non-existent right of way shown on the OS map, its line crossing lumpy ground and a couple of muddy ditches). ▶ Nearing a **sewage treatment works** cut left, parallel to the fence, heading inland towards a tall pole 300 metres away. On reaching it cross a footbridge and keep forward, alongside a ditch, on a good path to houses, there turning right to a road where you go left (rejoining the official route).

Turn right over the level crossing and pass caravans to reach Tywyn seafront. Turn left along the promenade.

The seaside resort of **Tywyn** is the jumping-off point for the narrow gauge Talyllyn Railway. Slate from the Bryn Eglwys Quarry was brought down to Nant Gwernol by tramway and loaded onto the railway for onward transport to the coast. The 2ft3in (690mm) railway ran from 1866 to 1946 and closed following a major rockfall in the Bryn Eglwys Quarry. The Talyllyn Railway Preservation Society

*In clear weather there are glorious inland views to Cadair Idris, Craig yr Aderyn (Birds Rock) and the Tarren hills.*

*Tywyn's beach, which stretches for 8km (5 miles) to Aberdyfi*

The village of Aberdyfi is one of the most attractive settlements along Cardigan Bay

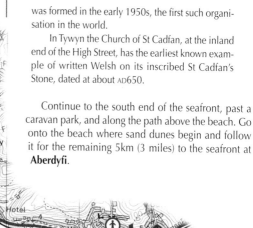

was formed in the early 1950s, the first such organisation in the world.

In Tywyn the Church of St Cadfan, at the inland end of the High Street, has the earliest known example of written Welsh on its inscribed St Cadfan's Stone, dated at about AD650.

Continue to the south end of the seafront, past a caravan park, and along the path above the beach. Go onto the beach where sand dunes begin and follow it for the remaining 5km (3 miles) to the seafront at **Aberdyfi**.

## ABERDYFI

In about AD78 the Romans were said to have passed through the Aberdyfi area as part of their military campaign. The site was also conveniently placed for the conferences between the princes of North and South Wales in 540 and 1140, and for the Council of Aberdyfi in 1216.

The first buildings, a few cottages, appeared in the mid 16th century. Aberdyfi grew as a port dealing mainly in slate and cork bark and with thriving shipbuilding. The Aberystwyth and Welsh Coast Railway Company's line arrived in 1863, but as the link to Dyfi Junction to Machynlleth was not completed until 1867, the first train had to be ferried across the Dyfi. As the port declined, and with the benefit of the railway, the town developed as an attractive holiday resort.

If, as you walk the sands to Aberdyfi, you hear the ghostly ringing of bells from beneath the waves, these are from the ancient and drowned legendary kingdom of Cantre'r Gwaelod, a sound called to mind in the 19th-century song *The Bells of Aberdyfi*:

> *'Pan ddof adref tros y môr,*
> *Cariad gura wrth dy ddôr;*
> *Mal un, dau, tri, pedwar, pump, chwech,*
> *Meddai clychau Aberdyfi.'*

> 'When I cross the sea once more,
> Love comes knocking at my door;
> Ding, dong one, two, three, four, five, six,
> Like the bells of Aberdyfi.'

# THE DYFI ESTUARY

## DAY 7

*Aberdyfi to Machynlleth*

| | |
|---|---|
| **Start** | Aberdyfi seafront (SN 613 959) |
| **Finish** | Machynlleth town centre (SH 745 008) |
| **Distance** | 19.5km (12¼ miles) |
| **Ascent** | 625m (2050ft) |
| **Descent** | 625m (2050ft) |
| **Time** | 7hrs |
| **Maps** | OS Landranger 135; OS Explorer OL23 |
| **Refreshments** | The Riverside Hotel in Pennal; a choice of pubs and cafés in Machynlleth |
| **Public transport** | Regular buses link Aberdyfi with Machynlleth via Pennal; there are trains from Aberdyfi to Porthmadog and intermediate stations, and to Machynlleth (continuing on the national rail network) |
| **Accommodation** | Pennal (guest house, campsite); Machynlleth (B&Bs, guest houses, hotel, campsites) |

This is a strenuous day's walking as the coast path makes its long inland detour to the lowest crossing point on the Dyfi. Having made the steep climb to the ridge between the Dyfi and Cwm Maethlon (Happy Valley), the path follows a quiet road with some excellent views, joining the Panorama Walk before dropping gradually back to valley level. Field and woodland paths lead to Pennal and the way soon makes the long, steady climb through a forest. There is a lovely prospect of rolling hills on the descent to Machynlleth by field path and excellent track, but care must be taken on the main road approach to the town.

See Aberdyfi–Erwpistyll sketch map.

◀ At **Aberdyfi** seafront pass around the **lifeboat station**, walk along the quayside and exit to the main road. Follow it rightwards and just after buildings on the right

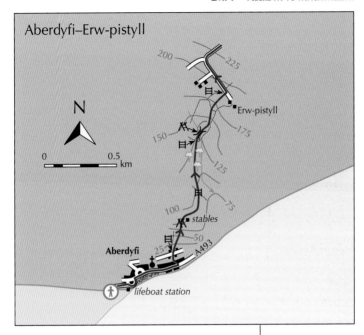

Aberdyfi–Erw-pistyll

begin go sharp left up a zigzagging path between houses to reach a road. Go right and immediately left up steps beside a house and continue ahead through scrub, keeping left at a fork.

Reach a stile by **stables** and cut right across grass to find a path entering some scrub. Follow this via a couple of wicket gates to a footbridge, then go immediately left upfield and through a gap. Keep to the centre of the next field and then aim left of the buildings of **Erw-pistyll Farm** to a wicket gate. Exit onto a lane. Go left to a road and then turn right.

Follow the road for 2.5km (1½ miles), with glorious views over Cwm Maethlon. The tarmac ends at the isolated house of Bwlch Farm. Continue on a wide track (the Panorama Walk). In one kilometre keep right after a gate, near a fence, beyond **Carn March Arthur**.

*Rolling hills dominate the view inland from Carn March Arthur*

A plaque marks **Carn March Arthur** (the Stone of Arthur's Horse). In nearby Llyn Barfog (the Bearded Lake) there lived the avanc – a fierce monster. With the help of his horse, King Arthur hauled the beast from the water on a chain and slew it, the horse making a hoofprint in the rock.

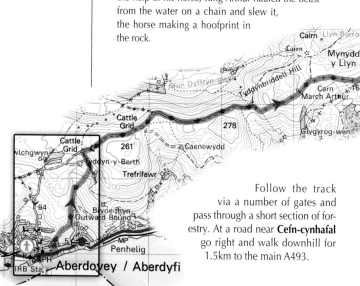

Follow the track via a number of gates and pass through a short section of forestry. At a road near **Cefn-cynhafal** go right and walk downhill for 1.5km to the main A493.

Go right and almost at once left on the tarmac drive for Cefn Crib Caravan Park. As the drive bends right, go forward through the left-hand of two facing gates. Follow the stone path half left, and as it curves left towards a gate keep half right across grass to follow a path along the edge of trees. Go through a kissing gate into a field and turn left, following an embankment to a footbridge over the Nant Cwm-sylwi, then half left to a kissing gate and onto a road. ▶

Go left and then sharp right after 40 metres on the tarmac drive to Penmaendyfi. Follow the drive between buildings of the 16th-century country mansion to a gate beyond. Climb half left in the field and go past an electricity pole to find a kissing gate in the top right

Note that the waymarked route between the A493 and this point follows a different line from the right of way shown on the OS map.

corner. Follow the path along the bottom edge of a wood and continue via two more kissing gates to enter a larger area of wood (part of Plas Talgarth Health and Leisure Club). The right of way keeps ahead through the trees to reach a wider path in 250 metres. The Plas Talgarth signs discourage use of this path, but could legitimately be ignored: it is a right of way! Alternatively, on entering the wood go sharp right on the Trim Trail path, descend some steps and turn left at the bottom onto a wide path.

Reach the holiday bungalows and other buildings of **Plas Talgarth** and follow the drive down past them. Keep on down to the A493, noting the castle mound

map continues on page 91

*The path passes the castle mound of Tomen Las approaching Pennal*

of **Tomen Las** on the way. Walk right to **Pennal** village and after crossing the Afon Pennal take the road heading left out of the village.

A kilometre southeast of **Pennal** there is the former site of a small Roman fort. The village church of St Peter ad Vincula ('in chains') is the only such dedication in Wales, founded in the sixth century by Celtic missionaries from Brittany.

It was at Pennal that Owain Glyndŵr is believed to have composed the so-called *Pennal Letter*, a copy of which is inside the church. Communications of 1404 and 1406 with the French king sought to show Glyndŵr's allegiance to Benedict XIII, the Pope in Avignon. (The English king at this time showed allegiance to the Pope in Rome.) The letter is in two parts, a brief one outlining Glyndŵr's intentions to show allegiance and a formal sealed document setting out, among other things, his terms for establishing a church and university in Wales.

Keep right at a fork, then in a further kilometre turn right up a wide forest road (National Cycle Route 8). Keep right at the fork in 700 metres and climb for a further 3km (1¾ miles). At a signpost, 500 metres after a forest road angles in from the right, there is a choice of routes.

## Forest road alternative
Continue for almost another kilometre to a junction of forest roads, where you bear right. In a further 500 metres exit the forest at a gate and walk down the rough lane. The official route comes in on the right in 500 metres.

At the signpost, the official coast path heads off right up the rough hillside. Almost at once bear right again and climb through scrub and trees to reach a stile. Head southeast downfield, keeping to the shoulder; do not get drawn into the valley on the right. Reach a stile at the far bottom corner and head down the lane. ▶

Follow the lane down to the A493 and go left. Keep well in on the right side of the road and continue to the Pont ar Ddyfi. Cross the bridge (beware of the traffic), leaving Snowdonia National Park, and follow the cycle path and pavement to the centre of **Machynlleth**.

The forest road alternative rejoins the main route here.

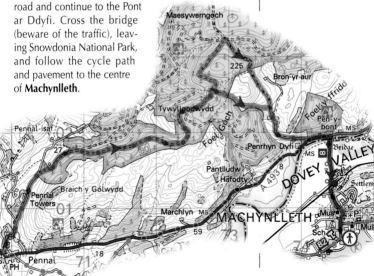

*Machynlleth's historic town centre is characterised by its famous clock tower*

**Machynlleth**, the ancient capital of Wales, at a crossing point on the Dyfi, was granted its charter by Edward I. This is the place most closely associated with Owain Glyndŵr (see The Glyndŵr revolt in the introduction; page 19) and there are claims that he held his first parliament here in 1404. The Parliament House on Heol Maengwyn (the location for the present-day museum) is, however, substantially a 20th-century restoration.

The town was a centre for flannel and tweed, and slate and lead were brought here for onward transhipment from the port at Derwenlas, a couple of kilometres away at the highest tidal point on the Dyfi. George Borrow, visiting the town on his perambulation through Wales, found Machynlleth to be 'a thoroughly Welsh town'. The buildings are mostly Victorian. The town's elaborate clock tower, gifted in 1873 by the Marquis of Londonderry, marked the coming-of-age of his son (the marquis then having his country seat at Y Plas, which is now in the town park).

# DAY 8
## Machynlleth to Borth or Ynyslas

| | |
|---|---|
| **Start** | Machynlleth town centre (SH 745 008) |
| **Finish** | Borth seafront (SN 607 890); or Ynyslas Visitor Centre (SN 609 940) |
| **Distance** | 24km (15 miles); or 29km (18 miles) |
| **Ascent** | 580m (1900ft) |
| **Descent** | 580m (1900ft) |
| **Time** | 8hrs; or 9½ hours |
| **Maps** | OS Landranger 135; OS Explorer OL23, 213 |
| **Refreshments** | The Wildfowler pub at Tre'r-ddôl (possibly evening only); various cafés and pubs in Borth |
| **Public transport** | Regular trains from Machynlleth on the national rail network to Birmingham and connecting stations, and from Machynlleth and Dovey Junction to Borth and Aberystwyth and all stations to Porthmadog and Pwllheli; regular buses from Machynlleth to Aberystwyth via Tre Taliesin; frequent buses connect Ynyslas, Borth and Aberystwyth |
| **Accommodation** | Borth (B&B, guest house, youth hostel, campsites); Ynyslas (campsite) |

This part of the walk returns you to the coast. If the distance seems too great it is possible to break the journey with a train at Dovey Junction, or at Tre'r-ddôl or Tre Taliesin with one of the regular buses back to Machynlleth. The walk follows the hill fringes east of the Dyfi as far as Tre Taliesin through delightful scenery, and there are wide prospects over the estuary and Tarren hills from the higher ground. There are several ascents and descents as far as Tre Taliesin, on quiet road, woodland tracks and field paths, which in places can get overgrown in summer. There is some tricky route-finding at times, so follow the map and directions carefully. The final kilometres to Borth are alongside the huge Cors Fochno bog, where walking is fast and easy, although after heavy rain the going can be very boggy here and there. A pleasant alternative is available.

The day's main route ends at Borth, where the Wales Coast Path (now coinciding with the Ceredigion Coast Path), heads south. The alternative finish at Ynyslas, which is a 5km walk north, is recommended for those who wish to ensure completion of the Ceredigion Coast Path.

The official coast path from **Machynlleth** follows the A487, but it is better to avoid this stretch.

### Recommended alternative via Glyndŵr's Way

*Glyndŵr's Way is Wales' third national trail, running 217km (135 miles) from Knighton to Welshpool via Machynlleth.*

Follow Glyndŵr's Way via the town park. ◄ Head along the main shopping street (Heol Maengwyn). Opposite the Owain Glyndŵr Centre and Parliament House turn right through the park gates. Follow the main path past the leisure centre and Y Plas to the park exit near the A487. Turn left through a kissing gate immediately past the park lodge (rejoining the official path).

Climb the Roman Steps, follow the path up, cross a stone track by the cottages of Cae-gybi and continue in the same direction to a road. Go left. In 300 metres Glyndŵr's Way bears off left, while the coast path continues on the road.

*The path leaves Machynlleth via the Roman Steps*

Look out for a stile on the right after a further 700 metres. Drop steeply downfield to another stile seen at the bottom and go right, then sharp left at a junction in 200 metres. Pass the buildings of **Troed-y-rhiw Farm** and fork right (straight on), still on a road. Pass the next farm

(Garthowen) and in 300 metres angle off to the right on a path that runs initially alongside the road. Continue via two gates, cross a sloping field on a terrace, and go alongside a wall to reach two facing gates.

Go through the right-hand gate. Descend through the forest for 1.7km (1 mile), eventually walking alongside the tumbling Llyfnant. Exit the wood and follow the path, soon a wide track, past the house of Felin Llyfnant. After 400 metres go left on a tarmac road, then turn sharp left at a junction and continue to the buildings of **Caerhedyn**.

Immediately beyond the house on the right, turn right through a gate set back from the road. Climb with the path via a second gate and continue up through trees, keeping close to the boundary on the right. Towards the top of the wood, pass left of a fallen tree to find a gate just beyond it. From here to the road the path can get overhung with bracken in high summer.

Keep forward, parallel to the boundary on the right, to reach another gate. In the next enclosure stay parallel to the boundary at first, but soon veer left then right through a small cwm to come alongside a wall. Keep alongside the wall until you reach a gate. Through the gate, go forward 10 metres then left through scrub. Pass through another gate and continue through trees to a road. Follow it to the right. In 1.5km you reach a bridge over the Afon Melindwr.

map continues
on page 96

95

### Link to Dovey Junction Station
There is a link to Dovey Junction Station here for those wishing to leave or join the route at this point.

### To the station
Just before the bridge go through a kissing gate on the right and into a field. Turn right and go to the top of the field. Go through another kissing gate and follow the grassy path ahead to reach a wider path. Follow it left and downhill through woodland. When you emerge at a gate by a house, turn left and walk down to the A487. Go left for 75 metres, then right by a brick house and continue along a stone track, arriving at the **station** in one kilometre.

### From the station
Follow the stone track from the end of the platform for one kilometre to the A487. Go left for 75 metres and then turn right

map continues
on page 100

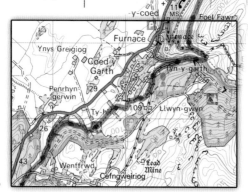

up a stone path to houses. Pass through the gate on the left of the first house and walk up through a wood. Topping a little rise, fork right and go down to a kissing gate. Go downfield towards the buildings seen below and before reaching them turn left through a kissing gate onto a road. Go right.

*The Tarren hills form the backdrop in this view over the Dyfi Valley from Foel Fawr*

Immediately beyond the buildings of Melindwr, go through the gate on the left and climb a grassy path through bracken. Continue on a terrace path along the slope of **Foel Fawr**, with lovely views over the Dyfi Valley and to the Tarren hills, to reach a lane. There is an optional detour here to Furnace, which involves a further 170m of ascent/descent. ▶

See Afon Einion–Coed Pant-coch sketch map.

**Alternative route via Furnace**
Turn right on the lane and follow its zigzags down to the A487. Turn left across the bridge over the **Afon Einion** to reach **Furnace**.

97

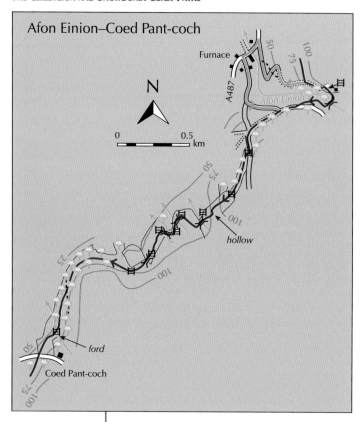

Afon Einion–Coed Pant-coch

**Furnace** is named after the furnace built in about 1755 by Vernon, Kendall and Co, West Midlands ironmasters. However, it was previously the site in the 17th century of the Ynyshir lead smelting and silver works. Ore from mines to the south was brought in by packhorse, the ingots going out by ship, mainly down the Dyfi. The silver was of high quality, so much so that Charles I sanctioned the establishment of a Royal Mint at Aberystwyth

Castle. For a brief time during Cromwell's siege of the castle the mint was moved to Ynyshir.

 The remains you see today at the site are thought to be the best-preserved example of an 18th-century charcoal-burning blast furnace in Britain, comprising the furnace itself and a building for storing the raw materials. It operated for only about 50 years, but was later converted to a sawmill when an original water-wheel was replaced with the present large wheel.

 Continue on the main road and almost at once turn left up the minor Cwm Einion (Artists' Valley) road. Climb steadily and in 750m rejoin the coast path at a wide track going off sharp right.

As the path across Foel Fawr reaches the lane, go left, then branch right at a fork and continue to a wicket gate near a house. Descend to cross a footbridge over the **Afon Einion** in the Artists' Valley. Climb right on a wood-land path to a road, and follow it right. In 40 metres, turn left on a wide track. ▶

*The picturesque remains of the charcoal-burning works at Furnace*

The alternative route via Furnace rejoins the main route here.

Much of the route onward to Tre'r-ddôl was specially created for the coast path. At a path junction go sharp left and in 100 metres turn right through a wicket gate. Follow the path through trees. Pass through a wicket gate. Follow the map directions closely for the next kilometre, as walkers have been known to go astray. Go right along the field edge and downwards; go left and right around a tree-filled **hollow** and then across to a footbridge and wicket gate.

Go half right across a field then down its left edge by a little stream to a footbridge and kissing gate. Walk left to a wicket gate in trees and cross a footbridge leading into a field. Go along its left edge to another footbridge and kissing gate, then walk along the right side of the next field to another kissing gate.

Follow the path through scrub and trees, crossing a wide track after 600 metres. When you reach a wicket gate and **ford** (the stream here might need to be waded across if it is in spate), head straight upfield to the top corner. Cross the road and head into the wood (**Coed Pant-coch**) along a wide track, which later becomes a path, through trees and down to the A487.

Go left, then left again into **Tre'r-ddôl**. The official route returns to the main road and follows it to **Tre Taliesin**, turning right before the chapel and following a back lane to reach a road, where it goes right.

map continues
on page 102

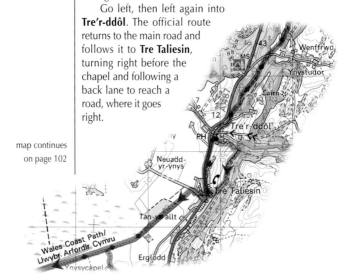

**Tre'r-ddôl** and **Tre Taliesin** lie in a former copper mining area going back 4000 years. Lead, silver and copper were mined in the immediate vicinity and the nearby hills in the 19th century, with hat-making also an important local industry at this time.

### Recommended alternative avoiding the A487

Turn up a bridleway before the church in Tre'r-ddôl, keeping right at a fork and going up to a second gate. Go right on a wide path and then down steps on the right after 100 metres. Follow the woodland edge and go down steps after 700 metres. Descend via a path and then a lane to the main road in **Tre Taliesin**. ▶ Head down the road opposite this to rejoin the official path.

*You may encounter waymarkers indicating a branch of the Ceredigion Coast Path, although its main start is at Ynyslas.*

Pass left through a kissing gate in 200 metres. Now follow a remarkably straight path for a little over 3km (1¾ miles), via various gates, through fields and woodland and along the southern edge of the **Cors Fochno Nature Reserve**.

*The vast bog of Cors Fochno, seen from a viewing platform near the path*

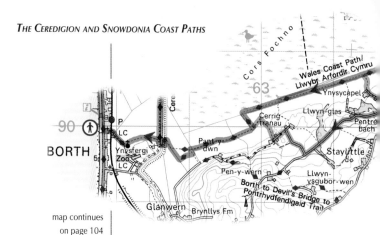

map continues
on page 104

An international Biosphere Reserve, the Dyfi National Nature Reserve comprises a mixture of habitats, including the estuary itself, the Ynyslas dunes and the huge **Cors Fochno** (Borth Bog). The raised bog, one of the largest peat bogs in lowland Britain, is clothed in a variety of sphagnum mosses and other water-loving plants, including bog rosemary and sundew. It is home to many species of insect (some of them rare) and to otters and adders.

In 1.5km, towards the end of the field beyond the first section of woodland, keep a lookout for a sign and map by a gate on your left (SN 644 906) indicating an alternative route to avoid a possible quagmire further along on the official route, pending repairs to sluice gates on the Afon Leri.

If the sign has gone continue on the path ahead, which ends at a footbridge on the left at the edge of woodland (not shown as such on the Landranger map). Across the bridge, follow the path south to a gate (this 100 metres can be very marshy) and turn right.

**Alternative route avoiding flooded area**

Go through the gate on the left, up a fenced grassy way to the white buildings of **Ynyscapel** and continue up the farm lane to a road. Walk right for 1.25km and take the

102

first road on the right. At the bottom, turn left through a gate signed for Cerrig-cyranau-isaf Farm. Pass the farmhouse and go over a stile on the right, heading down beside a little stream to a second stile and into a field. Keep to the left edge of two fields to reach a stile into the nature reserve and continue forward beside the fence on the left to rejoin the official route.

Go across a pasture to double gates. The path continues through the edge of wetland to a gated footbridge. Follow the field boundary on the left to a corner (ignore the footbridge here), then go north, still with a boundary on the left, to another footbridge. Cross the footbridge and turn left to a bridge over the Afon Leri.

> Under an 1813 Enclosure Act powers were given for the draining of the Cors Fochno and creation of an embankment along the Dyfi. The **Afon Leri** was canalised, which resulted in agricultural land replacing bog in a number of areas, as well as the rapid northwards growth of the existing Borth pebble bank.

Go right, then go left in a few metres via a wicket gate on a path leading away from the river. ▶ Cross a final footbridge and follow the path (near sewage works) to St Matthew's Church and a kissing gate. Take the surfaced path rightwards to a level crossing and pass between buildings to reach the main road in **Borth** at the seafront.

Those who wish to walk north to Ynyslas could stay on the path beside the river here (see page 104).

*St Matthew's Church stands on a rocky knoll among the marshes on the approach to Borth*

### Alternative finish at Ynyslas

Many walkers will wish to continue their walk from the northern terminus of the Ceredigion Coast Path at Ynyslas, 5km (3 miles) north. To do so, you could take the bus from **Borth** to the road junction at **Ynyslas**, walk north along the road for 1.75km (1 mile) until just before it ends at the beach, and then go left through the disabled persons' car park to **Ynyslas Visitor Centre**. To continue on foot only, however, there are two recommended options as follows:

- via Borth Sands **at low tide only**: where the coast path reaches the main road in **Borth**, cross over and turn right. Walk along the sea wall to its end and follow the sands all the way to **Ynyslas**. Keep a sharp lookout for a viewing platform set well back from the beach among the **dunes**. Turn inland beside a post with a flag. A route leads through the dunes to a boardwalk, via the viewing platform, to **Ynyslas Visitor Centre**.

- via the path alongside the Afon Leri: follow the **Afon Leri** north for 3km (1¾ miles). Cross the footbridge beside the railway. Go left on the B4353, re-cross the river and at once turn right to the boatyard entrance to find a track left of the main gate. Follow this to the Dyfi Estuary and follow the sandy track alongside sand dunes. Continue to the point where the road from Borth terminates at the sands. Go left on it, and almost at once turn right through the disabled persons' car park to **Ynyslas Visitor Centre**.

# THE CEREDIGION COAST PATH/ LLWYBR ARFORDIR CEREDIGION

## DAY 9

*Borth or Ynyslas to Aberystwyth*

| | |
|---|---|
| **Start** | Borth seafront (SN 607 890); or Ynyslas Visitor Centre (SN 609 940) |
| **Finish** | Aberystwyth Harbour (SN 581 817) |
| **Distance** | 10km (6¼ miles); or 15km (9¼ miles) |
| **Ascent** | 365m (1200ft) |
| **Descent** | 360m (1185ft) |
| **Time** | 5hrs; or 6½hrs |
| **Maps** | OS Landranger 135; OS Explorer OL23, 213 |
| **Refreshments** | Various cafés and pubs in Borth; beach bar at Clarach Bay and wide choice of cafés, restaurants and pubs in Aberystwyth |
| **Public transport** | Frequent buses link Ynyslas, Borth and Aberystwyth; trains go from Aberystwyth and Borth to Machynlleth (continuing on the national rail network) |
| **Accommodation** | Ynyslas (campsite); Borth (B&B, guest house, youth hostel, campsites); Clarach Bay (campsite); Aberystwyth (B&Bs, guest houses, hotels, campsites) |

The Ceredigion Coast Path starts at Ynyslas Nature Reserve Visitor Centre and joins the Wales Coast Path at Borth. Options for reaching Ynyslas from Borth are described at the end of Day 8. You may prefer to break Day 9 into two days: Borth to Ynyslas and back to Borth on one day (up to 4hrs there-and-back), then Borth to Aberystwyth on the second.

From the visitor centre there are two possible routes: the low tide route joins the beach and follows its course west and then south along Borth Sands. The high tide alternative also starts on the beach, but from there it heads southeast and follows the Afon Leri's straight bank southwards.

From the northern tip of the Ynyslas dunes there are splendid views up the Dyfi Estuary and north along the coast. A walk along the superb Borth Sands at low tide, or level walking along the banks of the Afon Leri on the high tide alternative, is followed by a mostly rugged coastal path along the cliffs, interrupted only by the unattractive caravan parks at Clarach Bay. Aberystwyth is a bustling town. From here, if time allows, you could take a break from walking for a day to enjoy a trip up to Devil's Bridge on the Vale of Rheidol narrow gauge railway.

For the main start in Borth see page 108.

**From Ynyslas – low tide alternative**
From **Ynyslas Visitor Centre** go through the disabled persons' car park to the road and turn left onto the beach.

At one time one of Britain's oldest ferries plied between **Cerrigypenrhyn**, at the northern end of Borth Sands, and Aberdyfi. A square hut on timber supports gave shelter to waiting passengers. When the Aberystwyth and Welsh Coast Railway Company's railway from Machynlleth to Aberystwyth was completed in 1864, a branch was proposed to cross the estuary mouth to Aberdyfi on a one-kilometre bridge, but proved technically too

## BORTH SANDS

As Borth Sands run northwards they broaden and terminate in vast stretches of sand, backed by a complex area of dunes, set among which is the Countryside Council for Wales Visitor Centre. This area is the Ynyslas Nature Reserve, part of the Dyfi National Nature Reserve. After the last phase of the Ice Ages, as the sea level rose, this whole area became a huge swamp. The woods of birch, pine and other types of tree that flourished here were inundated. With rising sea levels, longshore drift carried large quantities of pebbles northwards to form the narrow spit on which Borth stands. Cut off from the open sea, the marshes of Cors Fochno developed, and beyond the tip of the spit, less than 1000 years old, the Ynyslas sand dunes formed. On occasion, at low tides, the old tree stumps can still be seen.

In the dunes marram grass predominates, but there are also orchids and a variety of other plants and fungi. Butterflies abound in summer. The area is renowned for its variety of seabirds and waders (widgeon, greenshank, redshank and many others).

*A view at low tide up the coast, across the magnificent Borth Sands*

map continues on page 109

problematic. In 1865 the Aberystwyth and Welsh Coast Railway was incorporated into the Cambrian Railway Company. The line on the Aberdyfi side northwards had already been completed; following a parliamentary deviation bill, the line to Pwllheli was then built along the north side of the estuary and completed in 1867, the Dyfi being crossed near present-day Dovey Junction. Pending completion of this line passengers were taken to the Ynyslas ferry crossing over the Dyfi on a temporary line, usable at low tide. The wide path that is followed between the estuary and Steelkit (high tide alternative) lies along part of its route.

Follow the toe of the dunes, heading first north, then west, and finally south onto **Borth Sands**. (If the tide is fast-approaching look out for a decrepit brick hut on the dunes at SN 605 930. You can leave the beach here and turn inland, crossing a golf course to reach a road. To join the high tide alternative, cross the road, go between houses and then across fields to the B4353, reaching the Afon Leri near the Steelkit boatyard.) Continue along the magnificent beach, keeping seaward of the many **groynes**.

*A timber baulk makes for easy walking along the pebble beach behind the houses of Borth*

### From Ynyslas – high tide alternative

From **Ynyslas Visitor Centre** go onto the beach and head southeast (overlooking the Dyfi Estuary) to reach the end of the Steelkit boatyard. Go right of the yard on a wide track to the B4353, then go left across the **Afon Leri** and railway. Immediately bear sharp right on a path and soon re-cross the Leri. Follow its straight bank south. Just before reaching a kissing gate, turn right on a path heading across the wetlands (haunt of birds such as the snipe, reed bunting and redshank) and cross the railway, continuing across the golf course to the main road in Borth, and turn south.

*Before long on the latter, pass around a toilet block and follow the remaining length of sea wall until buildings begin on the right of the road, then go down onto the beach.*

*At very high tides it may be necessary to leave the beach earlier, at the lifeboat station.*

From the seafront in **Borth**, either continue along the sands or climb onto the sea wall. ◀ Follow alongside the backs of houses along a continuous narrow baulk of timber walkway across the pebbles. (Widening of the sea defences behind the houses means it is no longer necessary to follow the main road through Borth.) Cross the lifeboat slipway to reach a ramp up to a road junction at the very far southern end. ◀

> **Borth** stretches arrow-straight for 2km (1¼ miles) along the spit, where fishermen built their cottages and where boats could easily be drawn up onto the beach. After the arrival of the railway in 1864 the village that had sprung up developed into a little holiday resort, nowadays protected by a sea wall and numerous timber groynes.

The official route goes right along Cliff Road. The cliffs beyond can be subject to collapse, in which case an alternative route is available. Watch for signage.

### Alternative route avoiding cliffs

Go south on the B4572, leaving it along the lane at the top end of a small green, and soon bear off right through **Pen-y-graig Farm Caravan Park** to pass a farm and descend to beach level and the main path.

The main route joins the cliff-top path at the road end and passes the **war memorial**, commanding a wide view over Borth, the Dyfi Estuary and the Tarren hills.

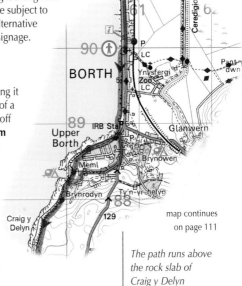

map continues
on page 111

*The path runs above the rock slab of Craig y Delyn*

*Approaching Wallog, with its isolated house, glacial Sarn Gynfelyn is seen stretching out to sea*

*The strata of the Aberystwyth Grits sweep up in a great slab against the Borth Mudstones, resembling, with a little imagination, the strings of a Welsh harp (delyn).*

At the seaward end of the caravan park use the zig-zags of the path – do not short-cut. Shortly after this the path passes above a huge slab of steeply tilted rock (**Craig y Delyn**) and the coastal scenery is impressive. ◄ The way to **Wallog** is obvious; pass to the seaward side of the house.

Among the residents of the lonely house at **Wallog** was George Griffiths Williams, Sheriff of the County of Ceredigion, who lived here at the end of the 19th century. He was also Commanding Officer of the Royal Cardiganshire Artillery Militia. Below the house, on an old quayside, stands a restored limekiln with Romanesque arches, where shipped-in lime was processed for the fields of the Wallog estate.

Easily visible at low tide is the long glacial moraine of Sarn Gynfelyn, stretching out to sea, it is believed, for some 11km (7 miles).

In a further 1.5km, at the somewhat bleak and unappealing caravan and chalet park at **Clarach Bay**, go past the beach bar building, cross the curving footbridge, pass the amusements and follow the road through the caravans. As the road bends left go sharp right on a wide path, climbing beside a conifer wood, and soon pass high above the rock stack of **Craigyfulfran**. This is a favourite perching rock for cormorants. On reaching the various buildings on **Constitution Hill** keep to the seaward side, dropping steeply and criss-crossing the cliff railway.

The great viewpoint of **Constitution Hill** is crowned by a café, toilets, a picnic area, an education centre and the world's largest camera obscura, the latter completed in 1985. The first camera obscura was built in Aberystwyth's castle grounds but later relocated. Most visitors arrive on Britain's longest electric cliff railway (237m/780ft), which has run since 1896 – the brainchild of George Croydon Marks, who later became a Liberal peer. The midway rock cutting was formed by excavating 12,000 tonnes of rock.

At the lower cliff railway station go right to the seafront in **Aberystwyth** and walk along the promenade.

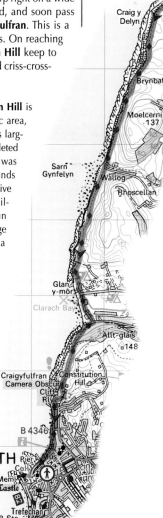

## ABERYSTWYTH

*Constitution Hill affords excellent views of Aberystwyth and Cardigan Bay*

Aberystwyth, strongly rooted in Welsh culture and standing at the confluence of the Ystwyth and Rheidol, is a pleasant town of mainly Victorian buildings, the largest settlement along the Ceredigion coast.

In about 400BC Iron Age peoples built the huge fort of Pendinas on high ground between the two rivers. The first castle in the area, two kilometres inland, was a ringwork-and-bailey built by the Norman Gilbert de Clare in about 1110. Edward I's later Aberystwyth Castle, built near the coast, was of an innovative design comprising rings of defensive walls, completed in 1289. But it was prey to the ravages of the sea, and even from the 14th century began to decay. In 1404 it fell to Owain Glyndŵr, but was recaptured in 1408. In 1637 a Royal Mint was established here and in 1649 Oliver Cromwell had it blown up, much of the stone being used for other buildings in the town.

Aberystwyth's economy was based on lead ore export, shipbuilding and fishing. By the time of the arrival of the railway in 1864 the town was already attracting visitors. The huge neo-Gothic hotel built on the seafront just north of the castle was, however, a financial disaster, but in 1867 a fundraising effort raised £10,000 and enabled the building to be formally opened on 16 October 1872 as Aberystwyth University. Today about a third of the town's population is transitory, with tourists here for a few weeks in the summer and some 8000 students here for the three university terms.

Aberystwyth is also home to the National Library of Wales, one of the UK's copyright libraries, founded in 1907. It holds over 4,000,000 books, including the *Black Book of Carmarthen*, the first book to be printed in Welsh.

If time allows, a visit to Ceredigion Museum in the town is worthwhile. Look out, too, for the town clock on Pier Street (restored to mark the millennium); the pier of 1864 and the church in Portland Street where Joseph Parry's hymn *Aberystwyth* was first played.

You might take time out to walk up to the 1852 Duke of Wellington monument on Pendinas, or, on a full day's break from walking, take a trip on the Vale of Rheidol Railway, which runs up to Devil's Bridge. This was the last steam railway owned by British Rail before it was privatised in 1989. Despite travelling on narrow gauge track of just 2ft (60cm), the locomotives and carriages are as wide as those for standard gauge track. Opened in 1902, the railway was built to serve the Rheidol Valley mines, transporting lead and zinc, and also timber and passengers, to Aberystwyth.

# DAY 10
*Aberystwyth to Llanrhystud*

| | |
|---|---|
| **Start** | Aberystwyth Harbour (SN 581 817) |
| **Finish** | The A487 road in Llanrhystud (SN 535 693) |
| **Distance** | 17km (10½ miles) |
| **Ascent** | 465m (1525ft) |
| **Descent** | 460m (1510ft) |
| **Time** | 6hrs |
| **Maps** | OS Landranger 135; OS Explorer 199, 213 |
| **Refreshments** | Inn and café at Llanrhystud |
| **Public transport** | Trains from Aberystwyth to Borth and Machynlleth (continuing on the national rail network); regular buses link Aberystwyth and Machynlleth, and Aberaeron via Llan-non and Llanrhystud |
| **Accommodation** | Llanrhystud (B&B, campsite) |

This is an enjoyable section, despite a couple of caravan parks, with excellent walking along a high, steep slope and above rugged cliffs and with a number of ups and downs. Almost the entire sweep of Cardigan Bay is in view and there are also great inland views.

*Aberystwyth Harbour, where fishing boats land crab, lobster, scallops and mackerel*

From the mouth of the Afon Rheidol in **Aberystwyth** follow the road around the harbour side. At the jutting-out wall (Rummers Wine Bar) turn left through a narrow passage, go up steps and turn right to the main A487. Cross the bridge and immediately turn sharp right into a yacht storage area. Keep over to the right, passing a launching ramp, to pick up a brick path along the water's edge. Follow it past a building to a road end.

Go forward through a fence gap, still by the water's edge on a rough wide track, and turn right onto a road over the bridge across the Afon Ystwyth. Walk left on a wide stone track at the back of **Tan-y-bwlch Beach** with Pendinas across to the left. In the 1830s, following levelling of the Tan-y-bwlch pebble ridge, a horse-drawn tramway brought stone from the Allt-wen Quarry to build a new quay at the Afon Ystwyth end of the beach. At the far end climb steeply up the hillside of **Allt-wen**. Continue on a splendid path, noting the several outcrops of steeply tilted layered rock running in lines down to the sea far below.

The path reaches a kissing gate near the corner of the **Morfa Bychan Caravan Park**. Head left upfield and then right to come along the top edge of an old field bank. Follow this up to reach a nice grassy track through gorse. At the access road to the caravan park go left and at once right through a kissing gate.

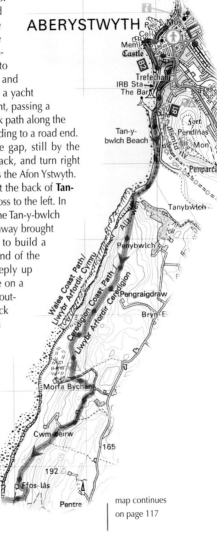

map continues on page 117

115

*Aberystwyth and Tan-y-bwlch Beach from Allt-wen*

**Morfa Bychan** was once a grange of Strata Florida abbey and in the late 14th century it was home to Rhys Ddu, a powerful ally of Owain Glyndŵr. Rhys was captured after the siege of Aberystwyth Castle in 1408 and subsequently hanged.

Follow the path steeply ahead and through an old field bank, which is then followed right. Continue into a grassy cwm and bear right, going uphill. Follow a fence to a kissing gate and rejoin the road for the caravan park. At once, by the 'Welcome to Morfa Bychan' sign, go right on an unmade lane. At the sharp bend go through a gate on the left (the third one along of four) onto a fenced grassy path.

Veer away from the fence 100 metres before the ruins of **Ffos-lâs**. Go upfield beside a field bank and then through a gap in it onto an old grassy lane. Fork off right where an old field bank goes off and follow it to the top of a rise, then go right and downfield on the obvious line of an embankment to a kissing gate. Keep ahead to the cliff and go left along a fence.

In the field approaching **Mynachdy'r-graig** go upfield to a kissing gate. Cross a stream, pass in front of the house and go up the lane beyond, very shortly bearing off rightwards along a fence.

> The strip of land from Morfa Bychan to just south of the house of **Mynachdy'r-graig** (Monk's House on the Rock) is comprised of poorly sorted boulder clay from the most recent of the glacial periods (the Devensian), and is less than 100,000 years old. The cliffs along this stretch of coast, being relatively soft, are subject to erosion and there are glimpses from the path of some impressive undercutting by the sea. The fertile soils formed from the boulder clay made this good farming land, managed as a grange of the distant abbey of Strata Florida near Pontrhydfendigaid, barley being then the main crop. The present house dates from the 19th century. In the cliffs just south of Mynachdy'r-graig, although not well seen from the path, is the Twll Twrw ('noise hole'), which lies on a geological boundary where friable rocks to the north give way to more resistant ones.

map continues on page 118

Look out for a stile and information board on the cliff edge off-route below the path: this is Tŵr Gwylanod (on the Landranger map near the words 'Pen Glôg'). ▶ Make the short detour. Over the stile a narrow and vertiginous path (not for the faint-hearted or in high winds) leads down to part of the hanging ancient oakwood of the **Pinderi Cliffs Nature Reserve**.

Tŵr Gwylanod, the 'seagull tower', is a rock cliff in well-bedded and jointed Aberystwyth Grits.

> A remarkable feature of the **Pinderi Cliffs Nature Reserve** is the ancient and gnarled oakwood, clinging to the precipitous slopes above the sea. The whole section of cliffs is rich in wildlife, including

117

a range of wildflowers and many species of butterfly. The cliffs are also the haunt of red-legged choughs, now, with help, becoming established along the coast. They are easily distinguished by their black plumage and orange-red bill and legs, and by their loud 'chee-ow' call, similar to that of other corvids. The birds pair for life and in this country breed in caves and crevices in the cliffs.

Return to the coast path. Soon, keep right at a fork to pass a large pile of stones. A short way further on, at a dip by another information board, there is a good backward view to the Pinderi oakwoods. In a further 1.5km, after a footbridge, the official route goes up to a high point and there is an alternative contouring path. At the far end of the next field,

*Stunted oak woodland hugs the exposed slope above Pinderi Cliffs, an isolated oak in the foreground*

where the fence turns right, go slightly left to a kissing gate to continue on the path beyond. A kilometre further on, below the cliffs, lies **Carreg Ti-pw**, a prominent sea stack.

*The caravans at Morfa; the path reaches an easier section between here and Aberaeron*

In the field beyond another footbridge do not head for the wicket gate in the corner, instead cut half left to a higher one and continue half left up towards scrub. Arrive at a crossing path and bear right. Keep along the edge of the scrub above the stark caravan site; at the end of the field bear right down to a roadway in the **Morfa Farm Caravan Park** near the shop and reception.

There is a small supermarket and café at the petrol station across the main road.

Follow the roadway left, almost to the A487 on the edge of **Llanrhystud**. ▶

### Extension via St Rhystyd's Church

If you are going to the main village or to visit the **church**, after passing the Pengarreg Club and old Pencarreg farm buildings leave the drive on a narrow tarmac lane on the left. The coast path can be rejoined by walking along the main road (pavement) to the point where the caravan park drive reaches the A487.

# DAY 11

## *Llanrhystud to Aberaeron*

| | |
|---|---|
| **Start** | The A487 road in Llanrhystud (SN 535 693) |
| **Finish** | Footbridge, Aberaeron Harbour (SN 458 628) |
| **Distance** | 11.75km (7¼ miles) |
| **Ascent** | 105m (345ft) |
| **Descent** | 115m (380ft) |
| **Time** | 4hrs |
| **Maps** | OS Landranger 135, 146; OS Explorer 198, 199, 213 |
| **Refreshments** | Pub off-route at Llan-non; good choice of pubs in Aberaeron |
| **Public transport** | Regular buses from Aberaeron to Cardigan, and to Aberystwyth via Llan-non and Llanrhystud |
| **Accommodation** | Llan-non (B&B, campsite); Aberaeron (B&Bs, guest houses, hotel, campsites) |

The walking is mainly easy across the coastal plain, partly on a pebble beach, and through a preserved medieval field system at Llansantffraid. There is an inland detour at Llansantffraid, should the Afon Cledan prove impassable. A particularly pleasant stretch across Clochtyddiau Pridd leads to the little village of Aberarth, the day ending at the gem that is Aberaeron.

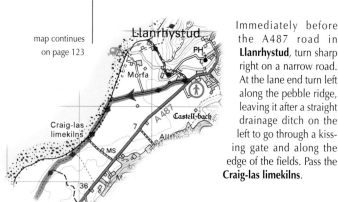

map continues
on page 123

Immediately before the A487 road in **Llanrhystud**, turn sharp right on a narrow road. At the lane end turn left along the pebble ridge, leaving it after a straight drainage ditch on the left to go through a kissing gate and along the edge of the fields. Pass the **Craig-las limekilns**.

The impressive row of the four **Craig-las limekilns** has an adjacent former coal store and beer house. Little remains of the rather makeshift jetty of stakes where the limestone, culm and coal were unloaded.

*Wooden posts punctuate the pebble beach near Llanrhystud*

There is a kissing gate shortly after the limekilns, beyond which the route follows the path inland, with a fence on the left. Reach and follow a hedged farm lane, which leads in turn to the church in **Llansantffraid**.

Until 2008 **Llansantffraid** was spelt 'Llansantfraed'. Confusingly, the Ordnance Survey now show both spellings, while some local sources have 'Llansanffraid'! There was shipbuilding here and elsewhere along this stretch of coast, with over 50 vessels constructed between 1786 and 1864.

The church is a Grade II* listed building, dedicated to St Ffraid (or Bride or Bridget), patron saint of dairy maids, renowned for her acts of mercy. The adoption here of the Irish saint may be due to maritime links with Ireland. The nave of the church is from about 1850, but features a late 15th-century rood screen headbeam. The tower has some

*A pretty cottage in the village of Llansantffraid*

15th-century (and earlier) materials. Many of the gravestones are of mariners, who travelled as far as South America. The village was the birth- and burial place of Henry Vaughan (1621–1695), a physician and metaphysical poet whose grave lies in the churchyard, his memorial inside.

*See Afon Peris–Afon Cledan sketch map.*

◀ Reach a quiet road, cross the bridge over the Afon Peris and go right and then left into **Heol-yr-esgob**, passing some pretty white cottages. Continue on a grassy track to the sea, through an area of long, very narrow fields known as **Morfa Esgob**.

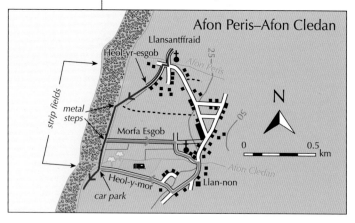

Afon Peris–Afon Cledan

Llansantffraid

Heol-yr-esgob

Afon Peris

strip fields

metal steps

Morfa Esgob

N

0    0.5 km

Afon Cledan

Heol-y-mor

car park

Llan-non

From Llanrhystud to Morfa Mawr the path lies across a level coastal plain of glacial deposits, which has unstable cliffs that are subject to constant erosion. Behind this rises the land that marks the original coastline. Extending from the sea to Llan-non is an area known as **Morfa Esgob**, divided up into 140 narrow fields, remarkable survivors of the medieval strip field system. Also called slangs or furlongs, they were farmed by serfs for the Bishop of St David's. When, for whatever reason, the bishop relinquished his hold in the area, they appear to have been taken over by the people who worked them, or maybe by incomers, and since there were so many landowners the original field pattern has survived almost intact through the centuries.

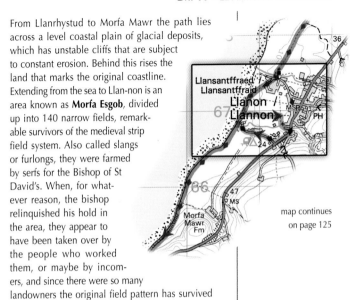

map continues
on page 125

Where a fenced path comes in on the left go down **metal steps** to the beach and continue along the awkward pebbles. Pass a second set of metal steps and continue to where the Afon Cledan spills across the beach. Paddle across to a rough **car park** (a difficult crossing if the river is in spate).

### Inland alternative

If the Cledan is impassable return to the previous set of **metal steps** and head inland on a fenced path. At a wide crossing track go right towards Llan-non Chapel, then keep along a tarmac lane past the chapel to the main A487 in **Llan-non** and turn right (pavement). ▶ Cross the river, pass a café and in 250 metres turn right into Heol-y-mor. Follow the lane to a rough **car park** at the end.

The church in Llan-non is dedicated to St Non, whose son St David was reputedly born here in about AD500.

123

*The path runs along low cliffs between Aberarth and Aberaeron*

The farm stands on the site of a former monastic grange. Henry Tudor may have passed through here on 10 August 1485 on his way to Bosworth.

Go through a wicket gate and continue along the field margin. On reaching a stream either ford it on stepping-stones or paddle across if the water is high. Inland is the farm of **Morfa Mawr**. ◄ The path soon leaves the level land for a while on a grassy path over Clochtyddiau Pridd. (If the tide is low you can see some of the fish traps that exist along this stretch of coast.)

> The **fish traps** are seen as low stone enclosures offshore, originally with wattle fences, where fish would be caught as the tide fell. That they are still visible at low tide all along this stretch of coast is remarkable.

Keep with the fence to where it ends at a low point approaching **Aberarth**, bear left towards the village and turn right down a grassy 'ramp' towards the nearest house. At a wicket gate go left to a second gate (not the path to the right) and follow the lane. At a junction go left, then in 25 metres turn right on a tarmac path and go over the Afon

Arth. Go forward and right, then right again at a T-junction. Continue, soon on a footpath, back to the sea.

Nearly a kilometre to the south of the settlement of **Aberarth** stands Llanddewi Aberarth Church, of 1860, on the site of a ninth-century foundation. Inside the front door is an old Viking hogsback stone, the only one found in Wales, which was used as a gravestone, laid horizontally to protect the grave.

In the 12th century stone shipped from Bristol for Strata Florida was landed at Aberarth, on land granted to the monks by Lord Rhys. There was also a Cistercian corn mill, which can be dated back to 1540. It is said the monks also extended the fish traps (*goreddi*) granted to them.

A great flood of 1846 washed away much of the village. The Victorian houses were built for retired sea captains. The arrival of the railway at Aberaeron in 1911 was the final nail in the coffin for commerce at Aberarth.

Follow the path along the low cliff, little more than a bank. The path soon continues along the back of the beach, along pebbles and through scrub, all the way to a car park and sea wall, which is followed to the harbour at **Aberaeron**. Follow the harbour side, rounding the inner harbour to reach a footbridge.

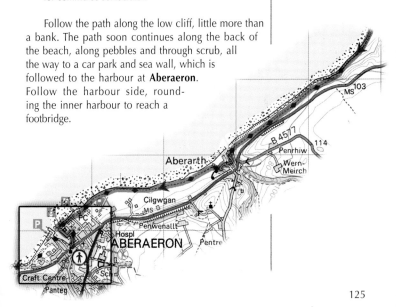

The colourful boats and equally colourful buildings of Aberaeron Harbour

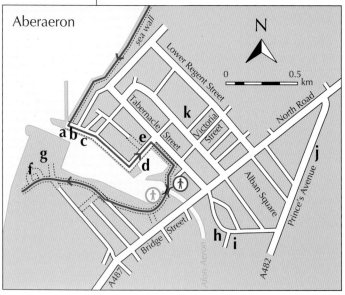

## ABERAERON

The little town of Aberaeron has a long history as a fishing port and of ship-building, with over 60 vessels built here. Aberaeron is a fine example of a planned township of small scale. The attractive core is Georgian. Plans in 1805 to construct a harbour led to the expansion of the village, under the guidance of Colonel Alban Gwynne and the architect Edward Hancock. Many of the houses were owned by local sea captains. Expansion brought many supporting trades, including a woollen mill on the banks of the Aeron and a local ironworks that produced the Aberaeron shovel. In the late 1890s a hand-powered cable car, 'the Aeron Express', took workers across the harbour after the bridge was washed away in floods.

The advent of the railway helped Aberaeron develop as a holiday destination. The town map shows a number of the points of interest to look out for:

**a** General storehouses. Former shipping warehouses, now Aberaeron Tourist Information Centre

**b** Harbourmaster's House and Spiller's Flour Warehouse. Built in the early 1900s and now part of the Harbourmaster Hotel

**c** No.3 Pen Cei was headquarters of the Aberaeron Steam Packet Company

**d** Warehouse and coalyard, now an ice cream establishment

**e** Milford House, home of Aberaeron ship owners and captains

**f** Lime weighing house. Used to weigh lime imported and burnt in local kilns. Nearby, on the coast path, is a plaque listing the many ships built at Aberaeron

**g** Enid Stores and coalyard. Coal was used for steam ships and in homes. Now the yacht club building

**h** Industrial area, once with a woollen mill and forge. The Aberaeron shovel (characterised by its triangular blade and long handle) was produced here

**i** Navigation school for mariners. Now a chapel of rest

**j** The cottage hospital on Prince's Avenue was originally a poorhouse

**k** Town Hall

# DAY 12

*Aberaeron to New Quay*

| | |
|---|---|
| **Start** | Footbridge, Aberaeron Harbour (SN 458 628) |
| **Finish** | New Quay seafront (SN 389 601) |
| **Distance** | 9.5km (6 miles) |
| **Ascent** | 225m (740ft) |
| **Descent** | 215m (705ft) |
| **Time** | 4hrs |
| **Maps** | OS Landranger 145, 146; OS Explorer 198 |
| **Refreshments** | Reasonable choice of places to eat and drink in New Quay |
| **Public transport** | Regular buses link Aberaeron with Aberystwyth via Llan-non and Llanrhystud, and with Cardigan; there are frequent buses from New Quay to Aberaeron and to Cardigan via Llanarth and the Synod Inn |
| **Accommodation** | New Quay (B&B, guest house, hotel, campsites) |

There are many rises and falls on this section, but the coast path is attractive, with the waterfall on the Afon Drywl a particular highlight. Further on, fields and woodland lead towards New Quay. The approach to New Quay will depend on the state of the tide: if the tide is low there is a fine walk along New Quay's sweep of sands. At high tide inland lanes and road must be followed. New Quay is an attractive little town, but the huge caravan park and holiday centre set above its cliffs are all too prominent.

Cross the footbridge and go up the far side of the harbour in **Aberaeron** to a road and head past the little lime-weighing house. Pick up the coast path at the back of the beach, parallel to houses. Where the houses end, cut onto the path running across the open grassy sward with the County Council offices across to the left. Just beyond, look out for a house with quirky architecture and statues. The onward path is obvious.

Cross the wooded Cwm Cilfforch. (This is the little wooded valley shown on the OS map between **Cilfforch**

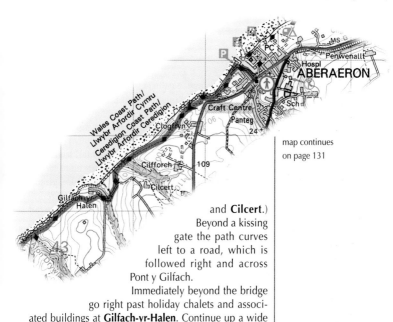

map continues
on page 131

and **Cilcert**.)
Beyond a kissing
gate the path curves
left to a road, which is
followed right and across
Pont y Gilfach.

Immediately beyond the bridge
go right past holiday chalets and associ-
ated buildings at **Gilfach-yr-Halen**. Continue up a wide
stone track via several gates. As the track heads southwest
look out for a kissing gate on the right. (The waymarked
route differs from the former right of way currently shown
on the OS map.) Go forward to a wicket gate (smashed at
time of writing) and then left to a second wicket gate. The
path is now once more parallel to the coast.

On the descent to the **Afon Drywl** do not shortcut:
follow the path inland to the valley floor and a crossing
path. Head right for 75 metres then left over a footbridge
(but first go ahead to a little promontory for the view of
the waterfall plunging over dark cliffs). Climb out of the
valley and follow the path along a nice grassy terrace.

Pass through an area of woodland (more than is
shown on the Landranger map). Keep straight over at
a crossing path, then go along the edge of fields to the
buildings at Llwynon (these are just before the road at
**Cei-bach**). ▶

See Llwynon–New
Quay sketch map.

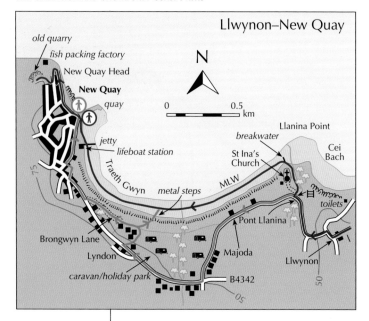

Llwynon–New Quay

Pass through the yard to the road and go right. In a couple of hundred metres or so a road to the right leads to the fine, popular beach at Cei Bach (Little Quay), but the coast path follows the road left, then right, to a bridge (**Pont Llanina**). After crossing the bridge you must check the state of the tide before choosing which route to take.

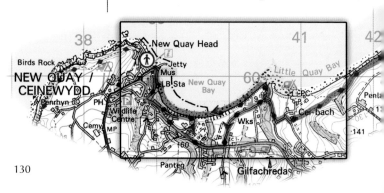

To check it, turn in on the drive for St Ina's Church. (To visit the church continue up the drive, bearing right.)

*The little church at Llanina is dedicated to Ina, a former King of Wessex*

From 688 to 726 **Ina** was King of Wessex. The story goes that he was shipwrecked in the vicinity of Llanina Point and, having been so well looked after by the local inhabitants, later returned and built the original Llanina Church, which now lies under the waves, lost to coastal erosion. The present building, possibly the seventh in this locality, dates from 1850 (restored in 1905).

Go through the wicket gate on the right and follow the path to the **breakwater**. If the beach is passable, you will be able to continue along it (see below). If the tide is high, or likely to be so, return to the road after the bridge crossing and go right.

**High tide route**

Continue on the road after the **Pont Llanina** bridge crossing for a little over a kilometre. On the way, pass the bungalow of **Majoda**, formerly a shack, one of the places Dylan Thomas lived when in the New Quay area. Go right on the B4342 (pavement).

*Fishing and leisure boats at New Quay*

Opposite a house named **Lyndon** turn sharp right by a gatepost onto a tarmac path descending through caravans and holiday flats. Below the caravans walk left and then right on the path. If the tide is now low enough it is possible to follow the path to the beach and reach New Quay along the sands. If the tide is still high, cut off up steps on the left, continuing on the unmade **Brongwyn Lane** back to the B4342. Bear right and in 200 metres turn right into Pilot Lane to emerge onto Glanmor Terrace next to the Black Lion Inn. Walk right down to **New Quay** seafront.

If the beach is passable go up and over the **breakwater** and follow the sands. Approaching New Quay along Traeth Gwyn, pass the **lifeboat station** then the left end of the concrete jetty. Go up a ramp from the back of the beach to a road and turn right to reach **New Quay** seafront.

**New Quay**, an attractive settlement of steep winding streets, takes its name from the quay built in the late 1690s near the present lifeboat station. Having been concreted over, however, it looks much more recent. New Quay developed as a significant ship-building and repair centre in the last 30 years of the 18th century, and also as a fishing port. There were at least nine different boat builders and some 240 vessels built at New Quay itself and at Cei Bach between 1800 and 1882. Rope for the vessels was made on ropewalks between some of the long ter-races of houses.

The various caves in this area were ideal for the smuggling of spirits and tobacco; it was from the watch kept by government agents on this coast that the Coastguard service emerged.

Dylan Thomas lived in the village from 1944 to 1945 and a good case can be made for believing that New Quay was the inspiration for the village of Llareggub (try reading it backwards!) in *Under Milk Wood*. If time allows you can follow the Dylan Thomas Trail (see www.newquay-westwales.co.uk/trail for details).

*The houses of New Quay rise steeply above the harbour*

# DAY 13
*New Quay to Llangrannog*

| | |
|---|---|
| **Start** | New Quay seafront (SN 389 601) |
| **Finish** | Llangrannog seafront (SN 310 541) |
| **Distance** | 13.5km (8½ miles) |
| **Ascent** | 690m (2265ft) |
| **Descent** | 690m (2265ft) |
| **Time** | 5hrs |
| **Maps** | OS Landranger 145; OS Explorer 198 |
| **Refreshments** | Seasonal café at Cwmtydu; café and pubs at Llangrannog |
| **Public transport** | Frequent buses from New Quay to Aberaeron, and to Cardigan via Llanarth and the Synod Inn; very infrequent buses from Llangrannog to Aberaeron and Cardigan between spring and autumn |
| **Accommodation** | Cwmtydu (B&B); Llangrannog (hotel) |

This is a generally strenuous and spectacular stretch of coast with some big climbs and descents. From the few houses at Cwmtydu to the Urdd Centre there is a somewhat vertiginous path cut as a terrace across the hillside, with no escape routes. An inland alternative via woods and lanes is available for those who have a poor head for heights, or in gale-force winds. The peninsula at Ynys Lochtyn is one of the highlights of the whole Welsh coast, and Llangrannog is surely one of its most attractive little villages.

map continues
on page 137

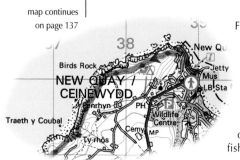

Follow along **New Quay** seafront and turn into Wellington Place, which continues as Rock Street. At the end (kissing gate) curve up through an old quarry above a fish packing factory to another road and turn left. ▸ After 25 metres climb up steps to a further road and go right to reach the coast path. Before long the path splits, there being a cliff option and a 'safer' inland alternative. Reach a lookout shelter above **Birds Rock**.

The quarry was the source of stone for the harbour pier, brought down by horse-drawn tram.

## CRAIG YR ADAR NATURE RESERVE

This stretch of coast has been designated as the Craig yr Adar Nature Reserve, home to one of Wales' best seabird breeding colonies. Some 4000 guillemots perch at Birds Rock from March to July, as does a large kittiwake colony from May to August.

The viewing shelter is a former coastguards' lookout, where, from the 1920s, they kept 24-hour watch in bad weather. The lookout fell out of use in the 1960s and is nowadays used during the summer to monitor bottlenose dolphins (*Tursiops truncatus*), which can be seen all year round off Cardigan Bay's coast. (They can also be seen along the Atlantic seaboard of Ireland and in Scotland's Moray Firth.) Adults can grow to between four and seven metres in length, and pods of up to 100 have been seen in Cardigan Bay. There are regular dolphin-viewing boat trips from New Quay, but some experts argue that this causes disturbance to these animals.

*Common Scurvygrass*

Although found elsewhere on the walk, drifts of Common Scurvygrass (*Cochlearia officinalis*), with its clusters of small white flowers, are particularly noticeable in the spring on the way south to Mwnt. Rich in vitamin C, this member of the cabbage family (not a grass at all) was used in the days of sailing ships to prevent scurvy. In the 17th century it was the fashion to take a glass of scurvygrass water every day.

*A dramatic piece of coast at Castell Bach*

The remains of the Iron Age fort have been severely damaged by erosion. At low tide this is a good place to see the contorted rocks.

In a further kilometre the path descends to the deep cwm of Nant y Grogal near **Traeth y Coubal**. Continuing on the obvious path, reach a flattish area of grass approaching the banks of **Castell Bach**. ◄ The official route passes left of the fort's banks, but you may wish to keep to the right for the dramatic view of the small island and cliffs. The path climbs steeply beyond.

In 400 metres look out for a right fork on the descent to **Cwmtydu**. At the road, walk along the little seafront past a limekiln and continue inland. Cross the footbridge by the toilets and follow the path up through a wood to a kissing gate at a crossing path.

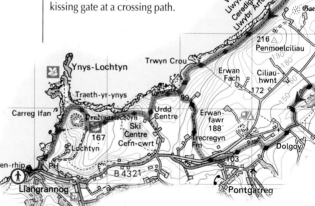

The tiny settlement of **Cwmtydu** comprises just a few cottages, a short length of sea wall above a little beach and a preserved limekiln opposite the few car parking spaces. This was a former lime-loading harbour, haunt of infamous smuggler Siôn Cwilt.

Now begins the climb to an exposed section of the coast path. There are two options here: in very strong winds, and for those with a poor head for heights, there is a pleasant inland alternative; if the conditions are good and you do not mind a bit of exposure you may wish to follow the dramatic main coastal route.

### Inland alternative

Turn left, heading downhill on the crossing path to a road where you turn right. Leave the road after 700 metres on a path descending into the wood. In nearly a kilometre follow the zigzags up and continue to a road. Follow the road to the left. At the first junction keep right, at the second go left and then turn right.

As the road is descending go through the wicket gate on the right, cut half right across a field to a further wicket gate and turn left. Pass to the right of a brick hut and down steps to the left of a house. Drop down the bank and head right along the bottom edge of fields to a road on the edge of **Pontgarreg**. Turn off immediately rightwards on a rising footpath. At

**Note** Due to winter storm damage to the coast path in early 2014, the inland alternative between Cwmtydu and the Urdd Centre must be followed until repairs are complete. See **www.walescoastpath. gov.uk** and click on *WCP Temporary Diversions*.

*Looking back up the machine-cut path below Penmoelciliau*

the top road walk right and then left into a field. Follow the edge to reach a farm lane and leave it on a right-hand bend at a kissing gate. Wind downhill to find a kissing gate in the fence above the cliffs between two sea inlets. Rejoin the main path.

The main route bears sharp right on the crossing path and makes the big climb back to the coast. At the top the path winds through old walls. It is worth leaving the path here by making a short detour to the right for the view down to Cwmtydu.

For nearly 3km (1¾ miles) the magnificent coast path follows a terrace cut in the steep hillside of **Penmoelciliau.** ◀

As the path passes through a kissing gate below the **Urdd Centre**, note the plaque commemorating the official opening of the Ceredigion Coast Path. The path bears left upfield. Before the Urdd Centre do not go out to the road but keep right within the field and climb through gorse.

*The hillside path was cut by machine especially for the coast path. Some achievement!*

The **Urdd Centre** (Gwersyll Llangrannog), founded in 1932 by *Urdd Gobaith Cymru* (Welsh League of

Youth), was developed to offer activities to young people from all over Wales and to promote the Welsh language.

**Ynys Lochtyn** lies below and the hill fort of Pendinaslochdyn is ahead. Keep parallel to the fence as far as a gate at a concrete vehicle track. Do not pass through the gate but take a path angling rightwards and downhill to the right of **Pendinaslochdyn** hill fort. Continue on a contour path, keeping left at a fork in the main path.

Ynys Lochtyn, surrounded by sea only at high tide, is overlooked by the prominent hill topped by the large Middle Stone Age and Iron Age hill fort of Pendinas Lochtyn (**Pendinaslochdyn** on OS maps), which was in use from about 500BC to AD500. The profile of the hill, peninsula and island is used as the Ceredigion Coast Path logo.

There are some wonderful quartz veins in the strata in this area, one of Lloyd George's favourite places for walking. Keep a lookout for the occasional red-legged chough.

Just beyond a seat take a right turn off the path through a kissing gate. The path soon makes a steep descent above Traeth Cilborth to reach **Llangrannog** seafront. ▶

The beach at Traeth Cilborth is cut off at high tide. Steps to the beach were built in the 1920s after two local girls were trapped.

*The tiny island of Ynys Lochtyn, seen here at low tide*

*A magnificent sunset, seen from Llangrannog beach*

## LLANGRANNOG

Sebastien Boyesen's statue of St Carannog looks down from the cliffs over the beach at Llangrannog where the saint is said to have landed in the sixth century. Winding up the deeply incised valley of the Hawen, Llangrannog is one of the most attractive settlements along the coast.

A dramatic feature of the main Llangrannog beach is the rock stack of Carreg Bica, a result of a collapsed cave. Legend has this as the tooth of the giant Bica, who offered a reward to anyone who could cure him of his raging toothache. It was the dwarf Lochtyn who came to the giant's aid: exhorting him to stand in the sea (one foot forming Llangrannog beach, the other Cilborth beach), the tooth fell out. In return Lochtyn's wish to live on an island was granted by the giant running his finger across the headland north of Llangrannog, so creating Ynys Lochtyn.

Smugglers used Llangrannog, stashing salt in the seaward of three caves in the beach cliffs. In the 18th century the many caves and coves along Ceredigion's coast were ideal hiding places for illicit goods. In those times salt was widely used to preserve food, and since it could be bought much more cheaply in Ireland it was regularly smuggled into Wales. The middle cave at Llangrannog, Ogof Fawr, is largely man-made, as it was hoped ore would be found there.

Llangrannog was the birthplace of the doughty Sarah Jane Rees (Cranogwen), born in 1838, who was awarded the master mariners certificate. She taught in the local school and coached local lads in the art of deep-sea navigation.

# DAY 14
## Llangrannog to Aberporth

| | |
|---|---|
| **Start** | Llangrannog seafront (SN 310 541) |
| **Finish** | Aberporth seafront car park (SN 258 515) |
| **Distance** | 8km (5 miles) |
| **Ascent** | 345m (1130ft) |
| **Descent** | 345m (1130ft) |
| **Time** | 3hrs |
| **Maps** | OS Landranger 145, OS Explorer 198 |
| **Refreshments** | Seasonal café at Penbryn; inns and cafés at Tresaith and Aberporth |
| **Public transport** | Very infrequent buses from Llangrannog to Aberaeron and Cardigan from spring to autumn, but regular buses to Cardigan and Aberaeron from Aberporth |
| **Accommodation** | Morfa Isaf (off-route near Traeth Bach, B&B); Penbryn (campsite); Aberporth (B&B, hotels) |

There is a great sense of remoteness to the first, strenuous part of this section, with one or two steep cwms to cross. There is a lovely wooded dingle at Penbryn and a spectacular waterfall at Tresaith, accessible at low tide. A surfaced path runs between Tresaith and Aberporth, where there are two linked sandy bays.

Walk along **Llangrannog** seafront, going around a right-hand bend. Leave the road on the seaward side of a sharp left bend. At the Iron Age fort of **Castell Bach** (yes – another one) the path makes a steep descent into the cwm above Traeth Bach, between the rock stacks of **Carreg-y-tŷ** and **Carreg y Nodwydd** (small path down to the beach) followed by a steep climb out. Continue into the field beyond a mast, where cattle often graze and the path is usually muddy. The route descends on a wide

map continues
on page 143

141

*Carreg Bica stands between Traeth Cilborth and Llangrannog beach*

This fine, long National Trust beach was used as a supposed site in North Korea in the James Bond film *Die Another Day*.

track through gorse scrub and then on a farm track to the road at **Penbryn**. Turn left and then right across a car park (toilets, seasonal café) and descend into a lovely wooded dell (note waterfall upstream).

Above a footbridge 50 metres beyond the top of the steps, the path forks. The coast path takes the left branch. (A further 20 metres past the fork on the coast path, where a path goes left, a short detour could be made to visit the little medieval church of St Michael. This path crosses fields to a road, where you go right to the church.)

### Alternative route via Traeth Penbryn

At the footbridge, the path to the beach (**Traeth Penbryn**) takes the right branch. ◄

At the north end of the beach look out for a flat rock, **Carreg Morwynion**, (Maidens' Rock), where, according to Samuel Lewis' 19th-century *Topographical Dictionary of Wales*, 'several females' drowned. The valley leading down to the beach is the Cwm Lladron (Robbers' Valley), a convenient route for illicit goods smuggled from Ireland in the 18th century.

To rejoin the coast path from the beach, return along the path as far as a flight of steps on the right. This leads to a path that can be followed up to rejoin the main route.

The coast path is clear, climbing gradually to a high point before making the steep descent to a road on the edge of Tresaith. At the road walk right to a junction, cross and go down the brick steps that start to the right of a bus shelter, and continue to the **Tresaith** seafront. At low tide you can detour right along the beach and round a headland to see the fine waterfall tumbling over the cliff.

map continues
on page 144

If you had seven troublesome daughters, like the Irish king of local legend, you too might set them adrift in a boat. However, having landed on the coast at what was to become **Tresaith**, they met

*The coast at
Traeth Penbryn*

*This dramatic waterfall, where the Afon Saith reaches the sea, can be visited at low tide*

and fell in love with the sons of seven local farmers, who they married and settled down with. Hence, so the story goes, the village name: the 'town of seven'.

Until relatively recently Tresaith consisted of just a handful of cottages and an inn. The inn owners, the Parry family, built their first vessel, the New Hope, at Tresaith, and later several smacks plied their trade in coal, limestone and culm from here. Tresaith grew in popularity as a holiday destination in the 19th century.

The fine waterfall was formed during the last Ice Age when ice still blocked the existing valley. Meltwater cut a new channel through the sand and gravel terrace, a so-called 'kame' (where the present-day caravan park stands) that had accumulated on the edge of the ice sheet. As the ice finally retreated, glacial debris prevented the river from regaining its original course.

Go left along the back of the beach to a path, climbing steeply beyond. The path comes back to the cliff and runs alongside a caravan park. For the last kilometre into Aberporth the near-level path is tarmac-surfaced as an 'Inclusive Access Path'. Note the several old railway carriages brought into service as homes.

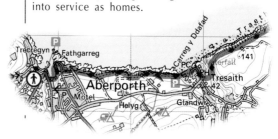

The path turns left by the first houses of Aberporth, then passes right of a car park and continues as a narrow road. Bear right at the T-junction, and from the road end follow the path down and along the back of the beach (Traeth y Plas) to a road. Follow it right to reach **Aberporth** seafront car park.

The pleasant and largely modern settlement of **Aberporth** lies above the valleys of the Howni and Gilwen, which reach the sea at the attractive linked beaches of Traeth y Plas and Traeth y Dyffryn (or Traeth y Llongau). In the 16th century this was a subsidiary landing port to Cardigan. The village grew in the 17th and early 18th centuries, with limekilns, coalyards and warehouses developing on the south shore. Aberporth became a centre of the herring trade.

The parish church is dedicated to St Cynwyl (in English 'Conwild'), a warrior-saint and a giant of a man born around 540, who, as the story goes, fought King Arthur at the Battle of Camlann.

*The quiet seaside village of Aberporth*

145

# DAY 15

*Aberporth to Cardigan*

| | |
|---|---|
| **Start** | Aberporth seafront car park (SN 258 515) |
| **Finish** | The Teifi Otter sculpture in Cardigan (SN 177 458) |
| **Distance** | Proposed route: 19km (12 miles); interim route: 19.75km (12¼ miles) |
| **Ascent** | 495m (1625ft) |
| **Descent** | 510m (1680ft) |
| **Time** | 6hrs |
| **Maps** | OS Landranger 145; OS Explorer 198 |
| **Refreshments** | Seasonal café at Mwnt; hotel at Gwbert; choice of cafés, restaurants and pubs in Cardigan |
| **Public transport** | Regular buses link Cardigan, Aberporth and Aberaeron; there are also regular buses from Cardigan to Carmarthen |
| **Accommodation** | Mwnt (campsite); Gwbert (hotels, campsite); Cardigan (B&Bs, guest houses, campsites) |

The path climbs steeply from Aberporth to make a wide detour inland, rounding a large Ministry of Defence (MOD) establishment, but from there it lies along a beautiful, rugged coastline, with the conical hill of Foel y Mwnt ahead and fine views to Cardigan Island. The walk passes above the beautiful sandy cove of Mwnt.

The cliff-top walk currently (2014) ends at a fence and field bank east of the Cardigan Island Farm Park. The coast path is planned to continue for a further couple of kilometres above the sea and then skirt the Farm Park, but there has been a long-running objection from the owner. If this route has been opened up when you get here, follow the signs and waymarkers: the proposed line of the path is indicated on the maps, leading to the drive of the Farm Park and out to the road above Gwbert. Otherwise the interim route must be followed, mainly on farm lanes and roads.

From Gwbert the path (mostly on roadside pavement) is along the estuary of the Teifi with views across to Cemaes Head. The last short section of the Ceredigion Coast Path, to the attractive market town of Cardigan, is mainly across fields, with views to St Dogmaels. (The way has been largely rerouted from that shown on earlier OS maps.)

From **Aberporth** seafront car park, go up the path back to the road by a dolphin sculpture. Follow a path parallel to the road, above Traeth y Dyffryn, returning to the road near a bridge over the Nant Gilwen. Follow the road steeply uphill and inland for nearly 1.5km, passing the **Parcllyn** MOD buildings.

*The life-sized leaping dolphin sculpture at Aberporth*

map continues
on page 149

147

Between the modern residential area of **Parcllyn** and the headland west of Aberporth is an MOD centre of excellence for defence aerospace and technology of unmanned aerial vehicles (UAVs). Since the RAF left, the site has been managed on the Ministry's behalf by QinetiQ, one of the world's leading defence and security companies.

Go right at the road junction and right again on a wide tarmac MOD access road (with a high security fence still on your right). Pass through the kissing gate on the left before security gates. Keep to the left side of a field to reach a kissing gate and then go diagonally across the next two fields to a wicket gate and footbridges. Enter a wood. ◄

**Note** The wood is not marked on the Landranger map.

Exit the wood near a footbridge and continue along the top edge of the deep glacial overspill cwm of Allt y Gwrddon, heading back to the coast. The path detours 'inland' around two small cwms and is thereafter easy to follow, going via several kissing gates and footbridges past the rocky promontory of **Pen-Peles** and in a further kilometre **Pencestyll**. Foel y Mwnt is now prominent ahead, beyond Hatling Bigni.

*The rugged outcrop of Pen-Peles*

*The distinctive conical landmark of Foel y Mwnt rises above a sheltered sandy beach*

Descend steeply to cross the stream below Foel y Mwnt. The official coast path heads half left of the little chapel to a road, which is followed to the right. (There are also paths over and around the Foel that may be preferred, although not in high winds. The Foel commands a great view west to Cardigan Island.) ▶ Leave the road 100 metres beyond a car park on the concrete path to the seasonal café and toilets. (A long flight of steps here leads down to **Mwnt** beach.)

Cardigan Island (Ynys Aberteifi), managed by the Wildlife Trust of South and West Wales, is home to a small colony of grey seals, lesser black-backed gulls and other seabirds.

map continues on page 150

149

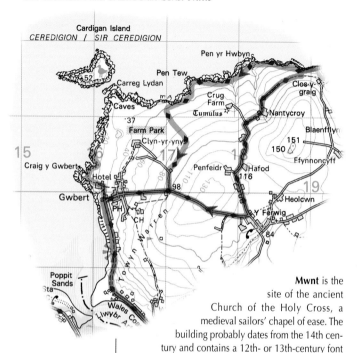

Cardigan Island
CEREDIGION / SIR CEREDIGION

Pen yr Hwbyn

Pen Tew

Carreg Lydan

Clos-y-graig

Caves

Crug Farm

Tumulus

Nantycroy

·37

Farm Park

Blaenfflyn

Clyn-yr-ynys

151

150

Ffynnoncyff

15

Craig y Gwbert

Penfeidr

Hafod 116

19

Hotel

98

Gwbert

Heolcwn

PH

Y Ferwig

CH

84

Poppit Sands Sta

Towyn Warren

Wales Coa

Llwybr A

map continues
on page 152

**Mwnt** is the site of the ancient Church of the Holy Cross, a medieval sailors' chapel of ease. The building probably dates from the 14th century and contains a 12th- or 13th-century font of Preseli stone. Mwnt is the site of a failed invasion by Flemings in 1155, a victory celebrated until the 18th century each year with a festival, 'the Bloody Sunday of Mwnt'. Below the side road to the toilets you may spot some grassy terraces. Hard to credit, but these were the proposed site of a caravan park!

Cross a stream and fork right. The cliff path currently ends at a fence approaching Cardigan Island Farm Park.

**Cardigan Island Farm Park**, with its motley collection of animals, occupies a sizeable area of land, including some beautiful coast overlooking Cardigan Island. Other than by visiting the farm there is no public access to the coast.

**Proposed official route**

The proposed route will continue along the clifftop for another couple of kilometres, crossing the cwm at **Pen yr Hwbyn** on the way before turning inland near **Pen Tew**. Follow any signage to reach the Farm Park access road, leading to the public road a kilometre from Gwbert.

At the fence, you must pass through the kissing gate on the left and head upfield to a gate. Follow the hedged farm lane. Bear left and then right through the yard of **Nantycroy Farm**, keeping right of the buildings. The lane soon becomes a metalled road, which you follow past a number of farms, including **Hafod**, to a junction just before the settlement of **Y Ferwig**. Go right and follow the road uphill, then down for 2km (1¼ miles) to the entrance to the Cliff Hotel in **Gwbert**.

At the entrance to the Cliff Hotel the coast path goes left along the surfaced path parallel to the B4548. (At this point there is the option of a 30-minute there-and-back detour north along the low cliffs, past the **Cliff Hotel**. Go right to the hotel, then left through its car park to pick up the cliff-top path along the edge of a golf course, passing the promontory – almost an island – at **Craig y Gwbert**.)

Beyond a car park **viewpoint** (which commands a fine prospect of Poppit Sands and Cemaes Head across the Teifi Estuary) follow the pavement alongside the road, passing a caravan park and boat club. In a further kilometre, as the road bears left inland and immediately beyond buildings on the right (Nant-y-ferwig), turn right on a wide stone track. Go through a boat builder's yard to a wicket gate, then along the right edge of a field. The way forward is clear through several fields, with some awkward narrow kissing gates.

▶ At a minor road, cross and go around the right edge of a field to a kissing gate. Pass through a narrow tree belt (via a footbridge) and keep along the right edge of the field beyond to reach a wicket gate. Turn left to a further wicket gate and follow a hedged farm lane.

At a road go right and in 300 metres turn left through a kissing gate. Follow the left edge of a field to reach a

See Approach to Cardigan/Aberteifi sketch map.

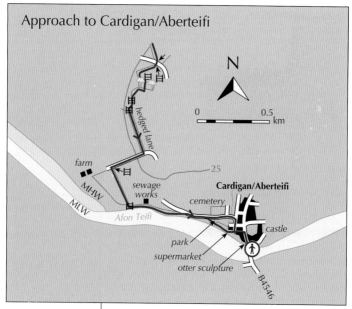

Approach to Cardigan/Aberteifi

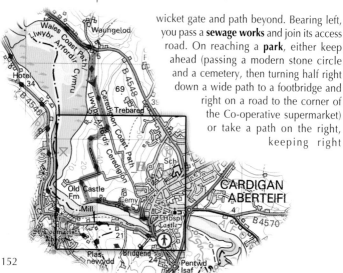

wicket gate and path beyond. Bearing left, you pass a **sewage works** and join its access road. On reaching a **park**, either keep ahead (passing a modern stone circle and a cemetery, then turning half right down a wide path to a footbridge and right on a road to the corner of the Co-operative supermarket) or take a path on the right, keeping right

*The otter sculpture beside the Teifi marks the end of the Ceredigion Coast Path*

at an octagonal paving feature, dropping down to a car park and going through it to the **supermarket**. In either case head up Quay Street to the main road in **Cardigan**, then turn right down to the bridge over the Teifi, where the Ceredigion Coast Path ends beside the Teifi Otter **sculpture**.

## CARDIGAN/ABERTEIFI

Cardigan from the bridge over the Teifi

Cardigan (or Aberteifi) is a pleasant market town, climbing from the medieval bridge over the Teifi. The castle was founded by Roger de Montgomery in 1093 and changed hands several times over the next 100 years. In 1136, after his defeat of the Normans, Lord Rhys set about transforming it from a wooden structure to a stone one, and a township developed, gaining its first charter in 1199. By the 1240s the castle was back in Norman control and the town walls, two towers and a new keep were built. Oliver Cromwell stormed it in 1645, inflicting extensive damage. In the early 1800s a mansion was built within the castle, which remained in private hands for many years and became derelict, propped up by massive steel buttressing. Funding for the much-needed restoration work was secured in 2011 from the European Regional Development Fund, the Welsh Government (*Cadw*), the Heritage Lottery Fund and the local councils, enabling the castle to be brought back to its former glory.

In the town itself, by the beginning of the 18th century a herring trade had developed and there was a sizeable fleet exporting fish, slate, bark, corn and ale, and importing coal, oranges and building materials. Shipbuilding, brick-, rope- and sailmaking were thriving industries. By 1815 Cardigan had seven times more vessels than Cardiff. The railway arrived in 1885; this, together with silting-up of the river, led to the decline of the port. Cardigan's railway station closed in 1963. As otters are found over much of the length of the Teifi, the charming Teifi Otter sculpture by Geoffrey Powell marks a fitting end to the Ceredigion Coast Path, where wildlife has been such a feature. The plaque reads 'Presented to Cardigan by Dr David Bellamy on behalf of the Dyfed Wildlife Trust to mark its Golden Jubilee, 1938–1988'.

# CARDIGAN TO ST DOGMAELS LINK

## DAY 16
*Cardigan to St Dogmaels*

| | |
|---|---|
| **Start** | The Teifi Otter sculpture in Cardigan (SN 177 458) |
| **Finish** | The Pembrokeshire Coast Path in St Dogmaels (SN 163 469) |
| **Distance** | 3km (1¾ miles) |
| **Ascent** | 70m (230ft) |
| **Descent** | 70m (230ft) |
| **Time** | 2hrs |
| **Maps** | OS Landranger 145; OS Explorer 198 |
| **Refreshments** | Pubs in St Dogmaels and café at St Dogmaels Abbey Coach House |
| **Public transport** | Frequent buses from Poppit Sands to Cardigan via St Dogmaels |
| **Accommodation** | St Dogmaels (B&Bs); youth hostel and campsite at Poppit Sands |

The route is mainly across fields and on lanes to the official start of the Pembrokeshire Coast Path at St Dogmaels. The way from Cardigan was once along the B4546, but since 21 February 2011 there has been a waymarked link path. Strong walkers could append this short link to the previous day's walk, or include it as the approach to their first day's walk along the Pembrokeshire Coast Path.

▶ From the Teifi Otter sculpture in **Cardigan**, cross the bridge over the Teifi and turn right on the B4546 (St Dogmaels Road). In 75 metres, between houses, walk left on a lane. Pass a cottage (**Parc-y-pŷs**), and after 100 metres go up steps on the right and through two wicket gates into a field. Walk up its right side. At the farm lane go left and then right in 30 metres to a kissing gate at the far end of the field. Follow the right side of the next field

See Cardigan–St Dogmaels sketch map.

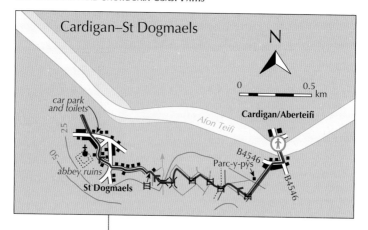

to reach footbridges and then keep ahead across the next field to a house. Walk down the lane to a T-junction, then bear right and left past the ruins of **St Dogmaels Abbey**. Bear left beyond this, back to the B4546, and left again.

The Anglo-Norman **abbey** in St Dogmaels/ Llandudoch was founded in 1115 on the site of a pre-Norman monastery by the lord of the manor, Robert fitz Martin, and his wife for the monks of the order of Tiron, one of only a few such

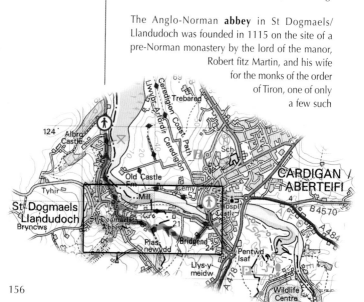

houses in this part of Britain. Excellent information boards at the abbey explain the layout of the site and how it functioned. You can find further information in the Coach House café.

Adjoining the abbey ruins stands the 19th-century church of St Thomas the Apostle, which replaced an earlier church moved here in the 17th century, which, in its previous location, had replaced a much earlier church dedicated to St Dogmael (named after the sixth-century Saint Dogfael). The Welsh name of Llandudoch commemorates the even earlier Saint Dethog, dating back to the Viking raids in the area in the first century. Inside, at the back of the church but poorly displayed, stands the important Sagranus Stone, which bears an inscription in both Latin and Ogham that holds the key to deciphering the ancient Ogham alphabet. The inscription reads 'The stone of Sagranus, son of Cunotamus'.

Pass the entrance to a car park (toilets) and in 25 metres, opposite the house called Almora, head right on

*The remains of St Dogmaels Abbey are well worth a visit*

*The Blessing Stone at the Netpool, where fishermen were blessed before setting out for the season*

a tarmac path, continuing as a lane past houses. Bear right and then left past a school and in front of the Teifi Netpool Inn. Take the left-hand concrete path (but first make the very short detour down the path, going half right to see the Blessing Stone).

> The stretch of river downstream from Cardigan was known as the Netpool, where fishing nets were dipped in tannin to preserve them, mended and dried on frames. Just below the Teifi Netpool Inn, above the river, is the **Blessing Stone** (or Answering Stone) where the fishing fleet would be blessed by the bishop.

Keep above the Teifi, returning to the road in 250 metres and following it right. The Pembrokeshire Coast Path starts near the water's edge in **St Dogmaels**, at a plinth in an area of green space, with benches and a mermaid sculpture nearby. Walkers on the full Wales Coast Path can now look forward to many more days of wonderful walking as they tackle this challenging stage of the route.

> Opened in 1970, the **Pembrokeshire Coast Path** was Wales' first national trail, most of its 300km (186 miles) lying within the Pembrokeshire Coast National Park. See *The Pembrokeshire Coastal Path* (Cicerone: second edition, 2003) by Dennis and Jan Kelsall.

# APPENDIX A
*Route summary table*

| Location | Distance from previous location | Ascent | Descent | OS maps per stage |
|---|---|---|---|---|
| **The Snowdonia Coast Path** | | | | |
| **Day 1** | | | | |
| Porthmadog SH 570 384 | 0 | 0 | 0 | OS Landranger 124; OS Explorer OL18 |
| Minffordd SH 596 384 | 4.5km (2¾ miles) | 110m (360ft) | 95m (310ft) | OS Landranger 124; OS Explorer OL18 |
| Penrhyndeudraeth SH 611 389 | 2km (1¼ miles) | 25m (80ft) | 55m (180ft) | OS Landranger 124; OS Explorer OL18 |
| Maentwrog SH 664 405 | 8km (5 miles) | 190m (625ft) | 140m (460ft) | OS Landranger 124; OS Explorer OL18 |
| **Day 2** | | | | |
| A496 Llandecwyn (nearby station) SH 621 375 | 8km (5 miles) | 345m (1130ft) | 355m (1165ft) | OS Landranger 124; OS Explorer OL18 |
| Harlech SH 580 313 | 10.5km (6½ miles) | 50m (165ft) | 55m (180ft) | OS Landranger 124; OS Explorer OL18 |
| **Day 3** | | | | |
| Llandanwg Station SH 570 286 | 3km (1¾ miles) | 70m (230ft) | 65m (210ft) | OS Landranger 124; OS Explorer OL18 |
| Pensarn Station SH 578 279 | 1.25km (¾ mile) | 5m (15ft) | 15m (50ft) | OS Landranger 124; OS Explorer OL18 |

Diffwys on the Rhinogs ridge, seen from Cerrig Arthur (Day 4; hill alternative)

| Location | Distance from previous location | Ascent | Descent | OS maps per stage |
|---|---|---|---|---|
| Llanbedr Station SH 579 268 | 1.5km (1 mile) | 10m (35ft) | 10m (35ft) | OS Landranger 124; OS Explorer OL18 |
| Tal-y-bont SH 589 218 | 11.5km (7¼ miles) | 60m (195ft) | 30m (100ft) | OS Landranger 124; OS Explorer OL18 |
| **Day 4** | | | | |
| Barmouth Harbour SH 615 155 | 8km (5 miles); beach alternative: 8.5km (5¼ miles); hill alternative: 14km (8¾ miles) | 35m (115ft); 10m (30ft); 545m (1790ft) | 85m (280ft); 20m (65ft); 530m (1740ft) | OS Landranger 124; OS Explorer OL18, OL23 |
| **Day 5** | | | | |
| Morfa Mawddach Station SH 628 141 | 2.25km (1½ miles) | 15m (50ft) | 15m (50ft) | OS Landranger 124; OS Explorer OL23 |
| Fairbourne Station SH 616 128 | 3.5km (2¼ miles) | 5m (15ft) | 5m (15ft) | OS Landranger 124; OS Explorer OL23 |
| Llwyngwril SH 591 095 | 8km (5 miles) | 335m (1100ft) | 320m (1045ft) | OS Landranger 124; OS Explorer OL23 |
| **Day 6** | | | | |
| Tonfanau Station SH 570 032 | 8.5km (5¼ miles) | 340m (1115ft) | 335m (1100ft) | OS Landranger 124, 135; OS Explorer OL23 |
| Tywyn SH 577 005 | 5km (3 miles) | 10m (35ft) | 25m (85ft) | OS Landranger 135; OS Explorer OL23 |
| Aberdyfi SN 613 959 | 6.5km (4 miles) | 5m (15ft) | 5m (15ft) | OS Landranger 135; OS Explorer OL23 |
| **Official route total** | **92km (57¼ miles)** | **1610m (5280ft)** | **1625m (5330ft)** | |

| Location | Distance from previous location | Ascent | Descent | OS maps per stage |
|---|---|---|---|---|
| **The Dyfi Estuary** | | | | |
| **Day 7** | | | | |
| Pennal SH 699 004 | 12km (7½ miles) | 380m (1250ft) | 375m (1235ft) | OS Landranger 135; OS Explorer OL23 |
| Machynlleth SH 745 008 | 7.5km (4¾ miles) | 245m (805ft) | 250m (820ft) | OS Landranger 135; OS Explorer OL23 |
| **Day 8** | | | | |
| Tre'r-ddôl SN 659 922 | 16.75km (10½ miles) | 560m (1835ft) | 560m (1835ft) | OS Landranger 135; OS Explorer OL23 |
| Tre Taliesin SN 657 914 | 0.75km (½ mile) | 15m (50ft) | 0 | OS Landranger 135; OS Explorer OL23 |
| Borth SN 607 890 | 6.5km (4 miles) | 5m (15ft) | 20m (65ft) | OS Landranger 135; OS Explorer OL23, 213 |
| **Official route total** | **43.5km (27¼ miles)** | **1205m (3955ft)** | **1205m (3955ft)** | |
| **The Ceredigion Coast Path** | | | | |
| **Day 9** | | | | |
| Ynyslas SN 609 940 | 0 | 0 | 0 | OS Landranger 135; OS Explorer OL23, 213 |
| Borth SN 607 890 | low tide alternative: 6.5km (4 miles); high tide alternative: 7km (4½ miles) | 10m (35ft) | 10m (35ft) | OS Landranger 135; OS Explorer OL23, 213 |
| Aberystwyth (pier) SN 581 817 | 8.5km (5¼ miles) | 355m (1165ft) | 350m (1150ft) | OS Landranger 135; OS Explorer 213 |

| Location | Distance from previous location | Ascent | Descent | OS maps per stage |
|---|---|---|---|---|
| **Day 10** | | | | |
| Llanrhystud SN 535 693 | 17km (10½ miles) | 465m (1525ft) | 460m (1510ft) | OS Landranger 135; OS Explorer 213, 199 |
| **Day 11** | | | | |
| Llansantffraid (for Llan-non) SN 512 674 | 3.25km (2 miles) | 10m (35ft) | 10m (35ft) | OS Landranger 135; OS Explorer 198 |
| Aberarth SN 479 638 | 5.25km (3¼ miles) | 80m (260ft) | 85m (280ft) | OS Landranger 135, 146; OS Explorer 198 |
| Aberaeron SN 458 628 | 3.25km (2 miles) | 15m (50ft) | 20m (65ft) | OS Landranger 146; OS Explorer 198 |
| **Day 12** | | | | |
| New Quay SN 389 601 | 9.5km (6 miles) | 225m (740ft) | 215m (705ft) | OS Landranger 145, 146; OS Explorer 198 |
| **Day 13** | | | | |
| Cwmtydu SN 356 575 | 5.5km (3½ miles) | 240m (790ft) | 240m (790ft) | OS Landranger 145; OS Explorer 198 |
| Llangrannog SN 310 541 | 8km (5 miles) | 450m (1475ft) | 450m (1475ft) | OS Landranger 145; OS Explorer 198 |
| **Day 14** | | | | |
| Tresaith SN 278 515 | 5.5km (3½ miles) | 295m (965ft) | 295m (965ft) | OS Landranger 145; OS Explorer OL198 |
| Aberporth SN 258 515 | 2.5km (1½ miles) | 50m (165ft) | 50m (165ft) | OS Landranger 145; OS Explorer 198 |

| Location | Distance from previous location | Ascent | Descent | OS maps per stage |
|---|---|---|---|---|
| **Day 15** | | | | |
| Mwnt SN 194 518 | 8km (5 miles) | 315m (1035ft) | 280m (920ft) | OS Landranger 145; OS Explorer OL198 |
| Gwbert | via proposed route: 5km (3 miles); via interim route SN 161 498: 5.75km (4 miles) | 100m (330ft) | 130m (430ft) | OS Landranger 145; OS Explorer 198 |
| Cardigan SN 177 458 | 6km (3¾ miles) | 80m (260ft) | 100m (330ft) | OS Landranger 145; OS Explorer 198 |
| **Official route total** | 93.75km (58¼ miles) | 2690m (8830ft) | 2690m (8855ft) | |
| **Cardigan to St Dogmaels** | | | | |
| **Day 16** | | | | |
| St Dogmaels SN 163 467 | 3km (1¾ miles) | 70m (230ft) | 70m (230ft) | OS Landranger 145; OS Explorer 198 |
| **Overall official route total** | 232.25km (144½ miles) | 5575m (18,295ft) | 5580m (18,320ft) | |

# APPENDIX B

*Facilities*

Places to stay – B=B&B; G=guest house; H=hotel; Y=youth hostel; C=campsite
Places to eat – EM=evening meals; D=daytime food/drink (may be seasonal, or lunchtime only)
Transport – NGR=narrow gauge railway

| Location | Places to stay | Shops | Bank/ cash point/ post office | Toilets | Places to eat | Transport |
|---|---|---|---|---|---|---|
| **The Snowdonia Coast Path** | | | | | | |
| **Day 1** | | | | | | |
| Porthmadog | B, G, H, C | ✓ | ✓ | ✓ | D, EM | Bus, train, NGR |
| Minffordd | B | | | | | Bus, train, NGR |
| Portmeirion (off-route) | H | | | ✓ | D | |
| Penrhyndeudraeth | B, C | ✓ | ✓ | ✓ | D, EM | Bus, train, NGR |
| Tan-y-bwlch | H | | | ✓ | D, EM | Bus |
| Maentwrog | B, H | | | | EM | Bus |
| **Day 2** | | | | | | |
| Talsarnau (off-route) | H | | | | D, EM | Bus, train |
| Harlech | B, G, H, C | ✓ | ✓ | ✓ | D, EM | Bus, train |
| **Day 3** | | | | | | |
| Llandanwg | B, C | | | ✓ | D | Train |
| Llanbedr | G, H, C | ✓ | | | EM | Bus, train |
| Shell Island | C | ✓ | | ✓ | D, EM | |
| Tal-y-bont | B, C | ✓ | | ✓ | D, EM | Bus, train |

| Location | Places to stay | Shops | Bank/ cash point/ post office | Toilets | Places to eat | Transport |
|---|---|---|---|---|---|---|
| **Day 4** | | | | | | |
| Barmouth | B, G, H, C | ✓ | ✓ | ✓ | D, EM | Bus, train |
| **Day 5** | | | | | | |
| Fairbourne | B, G, H, C | ✓ | | ✓ | EM | Bus, train |
| Llwyngwril | B, G, C | | | ✓ | D, EM | Bus, train |
| **Day 6** | | | | | | |
| Tywyn | B, G, C | ✓ | ✓ | ✓ | D, EM | Bus, train, NGR |
| Aberdyfi | B, G, H | ✓ | ✓ | ✓ | D, EM | Bus, train |
| **The Dyfi Estuary** | | | | | | |
| **Day 7** | | | | | | |
| Pennal | G, C | ✓ | | | D, EM | Bus |
| Machynlleth | B, G, H, C | ✓ | ✓ | ✓ | D, EM | Bus, train |
| **Day 8** | | | | | | |
| Tre'r-ddôl | | | | | EM | Bus |
| Borth | B, G, Y, C | ✓ | ✓ | ✓ | D, EM | Bus, train |
| **The Ceredigion Coast Path** | | | | | | |
| **Day 9** | | | | | | |
| Ynyslas | C | | | ✓ | | Bus |
| Borth | B, G, Y, C | ✓ | ✓ | ✓ | D, EM | Bus, train |
| Clarach | C | | | ✓ | D, EM | Bus |
| Constitution Hill | | | | ✓ | D | |
| Aberystwyth | B, G, H, C | ✓ | ✓ | ✓ | D, EM | Bus, train |

| Location | Places to stay | Shops | Bank/cash point/post office | Toilets | Places to eat | Transport |
|---|---|---|---|---|---|---|
| **Day 10** | | | | | | |
| Llanrhystud | B, C | ✓ | ✓ | | D, EM | Bus |
| **Day 11** | | | | | | |
| Llan-non | B, C | ✓ | ✓ | | D, EM | Bus |
| Aberaeron | B, G, H, C | ✓ | ✓ | ✓ | D, EM | Bus |
| **Day 12** | | | | | | |
| New Quay | B, G, H, C | ✓ | ✓ | ✓ | D, EM | Bus |
| **Day 13** | | | | | | |
| Cwmtydu | B | | | ✓ | D | |
| Llangrannog | H | ✓ | | ✓ | D, EM | Bus (summer only) |
| **Day 14** | | | | | | |
| Morfa Isaf (off-route) | B | | | | | |
| Penbryn | C | | | ✓ | D | |
| Tresaith | | | | ✓ | D | |
| Aberporth | B, H | ✓ | ✓ | ✓ | D, EM | Bus |
| **Day 15** | | | | | | |
| Mwnt | C | | | ✓ | D | |
| Gwbert | H, C | | | | D, EM | Bus (occasional) |
| Cardigan | B, G, C | ✓ | ✓ | ✓ | D, EM | Bus |
| **Cardigan to St Dogmaels** | | | | | | |
| **Day 16** | | | | | | |
| St Dogmaels | B, Y, C | ✓ | ✓ | ✓ | D, EM | Bus |

# APPENDIX C
*Useful contacts*

The seafront at Tywyn (Day 6)

**Tourist Information Centres**

Aberaeron TIC
The Quay
Aberaeron
Ceredigion
SA46 0BT
Tel. 01545 570602
Email: aberaerontic@ceredigion.gov.uk

Aberdyfi TIC
The Wharf Gardens
Aberdyfi
Gwynedd
LL35 0EE
Tel. 01654 767321
Email: tic.aberdyfi@eryri-npa.gov.uk

Aberystwyth TIC
Terrace Road
Aberystwyth
Ceredigion
SY23 2AG
Tel. 01970 612125
Email: aberystwythtic@ceredigion.gov.uk

Barmouth TIC
The Station
Station Road
Barmouth
Gwynedd
LL42 1LU
Tel. 01341 280787
Email: barmouth.tic@gwynedd.gov.uk

Borth TIC (seasonal opening only)
Cambrian Terrace
Borth
Ceredigion
SY24 5HY
Tel. 01970 871174
Email: borthtic@ceredigion.gov.uk

Cardigan TIC
Theatr Mwldan
Bath House Road
Cardigan
Ceredigion
SA43 1JY
Tel. 01239 613230
Email: cardigantic@ceredigion.gov.uk

Harlech TIC
Llys y Graig
High Street
Harlech
LL46 2YE

Tel. 01766 780658
Email: tic.harlech@eryri-npa.gov.uk

New Quay TIC
Church Street
New Quay
Ceredigion
SA45 9NZ
Tel. 01545 560865
Email: newquaytic@ceredigion.gov.uk

Porthmadog TIC
High Street
Porthmadog
Gwynedd
LL49 9LP
Tel. 01766 512981
Email: porthmadog.tic@gwynedd.gov.uk

*The conical hill of Foel y Mwnt seen beyond Hatling Bigni (Day 15)*

The Tarren hills seen across the Afon Leri (Day 9)

Tywyn TIC
High Street
Tywyn
Gwynedd
LL36 9AD
Tel. 01654 710070
Email: tywyn.tic@gwynedd.gov.uk

**Local authorities**
Countryside Council for Wales
Maes y Ffynnon
Penrhosgarnedd
Bangor
Gwynedd
LL57 2DW
Tel. 0845 1306229
Email: enquiries@ccw.gov.uk

Snowdonia National Park Authority
National Park Offices
Penrhyndeudraeth
Gwynedd
LL48 6LF
Tel. 01766 770274
Email: parc@snowdonia-npa.gov.uk

Gwynedd County Council
Council Offices
Shirehall Street
Caernarfon
Gwynedd
LL55 1SH
Tel. 01766 771000

Ceredigion County Council
Penmorfa
Aberaeron
Ceredigion
SA46 0PA
Tel. 01545 570881

Pembrokeshire County Council
County Hall
Haverfordwest
Pembrokeshire
SA61 1TP
Tel. 01437 764551
Email: enquiries@pembrokeshire.gov.uk

Powys County Council
County Hall
Llandrindod Wells
Powys
LD1 5LG
Tel. 0845 602 7030

**Travel**
Traveline Cymru
Tel. 0871 200 2233
www.traveline-cymru.info
(An excellent general site for planning
your journeys to or within Wales.)

Arriva Trains
Tel. 0845 606 1660
www.arrivatrainswales.co.uk

National Express
Tel. 08717 818178
www.nationalexpress.com

Cardi Bach bus
Tel. 0845 686 0242
www.ceredigioncoastpath.org.uk/
cardi-bach

# LISTING OF CICERONE GUIDES

Roads and Tracks of the
    Lake District
Rocky Rambler's Wild Walks
Scrambles in the Lake District
    North & South
Short Walks in Lakeland
    1 South Lakeland
    2 North Lakeland
    3 West Lakeland
The Cumbria Coastal Way
The Cumbria Way and the
    Allerdale Ramble
Tour of the Lake District

**DERBYSHIRE, PEAK DISTRICT
AND MIDLANDS**
High Peak Walks
Scrambles in the Dark Peak
The Star Family Walks
Walking in Derbyshire
White Peak Walks
    The Northern Dales
    The Southern Dales

**SOUTHERN ENGLAND**
Suffolk Coast & Heaths Walks
The Cotswold Way
The North Downs Way
The Peddars Way and Norfolk
    Coast Path
The Ridgeway National Trail
The South Downs Way
The South West Coast Path
The Thames Path
Walking in Berkshire
Walking in Essex
Walking in Kent
Walking in Norfolk
Walking in Sussex
Walking in the Cotswolds
Walking in the Isles of Scilly
Walking in the New Forest
Walking in the Thames Valley
Walking on Dartmoor
Walking on Guernsey
Walking on Jersey
Walking on the Isle of Wight
Walks in the South Downs
    National Park

**WALES AND WELSH BORDERS**
Backpacker's Britain – Wales
Glyndwr's Way
Great Mountain Days
    in Snowdonia
Hillwalking in Snowdonia

Hillwalking in Wales: 1&2
Offa's Dyke Path
Ridges of Snowdonia
Scrambles in Snowdonia
The Ascent of Snowdon
The Ceredigion and Snowdonia
    Coast Paths
Lleyn Peninsula Coastal Path
Pembrokeshire Coastal Path
The Severn Way
The Shropshire Hills
The Wye Valley Walk
Walking in Pembrokeshire
Walking in the Forest of Dean
Walking in the South
    Wales Valleys
Walking on Gower
Walking on the Brecon Beacons
Welsh Winter Climbs

**INTERNATIONAL
CHALLENGES, COLLECTIONS
AND ACTIVITIES**
Canyoning
Europe's High Points
The Via Francigena
    (Canterbury to Rome): 1&2

**EUROPEAN CYCLING**
Cycle Touring in France
Cycle Touring in Ireland
Cycle Touring in Spain
Cycle Touring in Switzerland
Cycling in the French Alps
Cycling the Canal du Midi
Cycling the River Loire
The Danube Cycleway
The Grand Traverse of the
    Massif Central
The Rhine Cycle Route
The Way of St James

**AFRICA**
Climbing in the Moroccan
    Anti-Atlas
Kilimanjaro
Mountaineering in the Moroccan
    High Atlas
The High Atlas
Trekking in the Atlas Mountains
Walking in the Drakensberg

**ALPS – CROSS-BORDER
ROUTES**
100 Hut Walks in the Alps
Across the Eastern Alps: E5

Alpine Points of View
Alpine Ski Mountaineering
    1 Western Alps
    2 Central and Eastern Alps
Chamonix to Zermatt
Snowshoeing
Tour of Mont Blanc
Tour of Monte Rosa
Tour of the Matterhorn
Trekking in the Alps
Trekking in the Silvretta and
    Rätikon Alps
Walking in the Alps
Walks and Treks in the
    Maritime Alps

**PYRENEES AND FRANCE/SPAIN
CROSS-BORDER ROUTES**
Rock Climbs in the Pyrenees
The GR10 Trail
The Mountains of Andorra
The Pyrenean Haute Route
The Pyrenees
The Way of St James
Through the Spanish Pyrenees:
    GR11
Walks and Climbs in the Pyrenees

**AUSTRIA**
The Adlerweg
Trekking in Austria's Hohe Tauern
Trekking in the Stubai Alps
Trekking in the Zillertal Alps
Walking in Austria

**EASTERN EUROPE**
The High Tatras
The Mountains of Romania
Walking in Bulgaria's
    National Parks
Walking in Hungary

**FRANCE**
Chamonix Mountain Adventures
Ecrins National Park
GR20: Corsica
Mont Blanc Walks
Mountain Adventures in
    the Maurienne
The Cathar Way
The GR5 Trail
The Robert Louis Stevenson Trail
Tour of the Oisans: The GR54
Tour of the Queyras
Tour of the Vanoise

For full information on all our guides, and to order books and eBooks, visit our website: **www.cicerone.co.uk**.

## Walking – Trekking – Mountaineering – Climbing – Cycling

**Over 40 years, Cicerone have built up an outstanding collection of 300 guides, inspiring all sorts of amazing adventures.**

Every guide comes from extensive exploration and research by our expert authors, all with a passion for their subjects. They are frequently praised, endorsed and used by clubs, instructors and outdoor organisations.

All our titles can now be bought as **e-books** and many as iPad and Kindle files and we will continue to make all our guides available for these and many other devices.

Our website shows any **new information** we've received since a book was published. Please do let us know if you find anything has changed, so that we can pass on the latest details. On our **website** you'll also find some great ideas and lots of information, including sample chapters, contents lists, reviews, articles and a photo gallery.

It's easy to keep in touch with what's going on at Cicerone, by getting our monthly **free e-newsletter**, which is full of offers, competitions, up-to-date information and topical articles. You can subscribe on our home page and also follow us on **Facebook** and **Twitter**, as well as our **blog**.

**Cicerone – the very best guides for exploring the world.**

# CICERONE

2 Police Square  Milnthorpe  Cumbria  LA7 7PY
Tel: 015395 62069  info@cicerone.co.uk
**www.cicerone.co.uk**